WHEN LIFE IS UNFAIR

WHEN
LIFE
IS
UNFAIR
Larry Richards

WORD PUBLISHING
Dallas · London · Sydney · Singapore

WHEN LIFE IS UNFAIR: FEELING GOD'S PRESENCE

Unless otherwise indicated, Scripture quotations in this book are from The Holy Bible, New International Version (NIV). Copyright © 1973, 1978, 1984 International Bible Society. Used by permission of Zondervan Bible Publishers.

Library of Congress Cataloging-in-Publication Data:

Richards, Larry, 1931–
    When Life Is Unfair: feeling God's presence / Larry Richards.
        p.   cm.
    ISBN 0-8499-0665-2
    1. Suffering—Religious aspects—Christianity.   2. Consolation.
I. Title.
BT732.7.R54 1989
248.8'6—dc20   89-14841
                                                                         CIP

Printed in the United States of America
9 8 0 1 2 3 9 BKC 9 8 7 6 5 4 3 2

This series is for Sue

Contents

Shout for joy to the Lord, all the earth.
   Serve the Lord with gladness;
   come before him with joyful songs.
Know that the Lord is God.
   It is he who made us, and we are his;
   we are his people, the sheep of his pasture.

Enter his gates with thanksgiving
   and his courts with praise;
   give thanks to him and praise his name.

For the Lord is good and his love endures forever;
   his faithfulness continues through all generations.

Psalm 100 NIV

A Personal Word

Psalm 100 is warm. It is consoling. It's like the down comforter my mother had when I was a child. If I was cold, or lonely, or afraid, Mom would throw the comforter over my bed, and sit with me for a while. I'd snuggle up against her and pull the comforter up around my neck. It was so soft, so warm, I could lose myself in its folds.

Psalm 100 is like this. It's a down comforter you can pull up around you when you're cold or lonely or afraid. Just read the words, and feel the warmth. The Lord is God. It is he who made us, and we are his. We are his people. We are the sheep of his pasture. The Lord is good. His love endures forever. His faithfulness continues through all generations.

The trouble is, there are times when we're too cold to be warmed by the most comforting of words—times when we feel too vulnerable, too alone, too afraid. These are the times when events force us to face the grim fact that, though God may be good, life isn't fair. God may be Lord, but bad things do happen to his people.

This book is written for just such times—times when we are overwhelmed by the "wrongness" of things that happen to us, to our loved ones, or even to people we read about in the newspaper. *When Life Is Unfair* takes an honest look at the "wrong" things that happen to people in this world. It also looks into the Scriptures, to search out incidents and principles that enable men and women of faith to affirm God's goodness even when he seems most hidden by the darkness that presses in around them. Each chapter, an independent meditation, is an invitation to see life's unfairness in a fresh, new way.

I hope you'll want to share your exploration of *When Life Is Unfair* with others, perhaps in Sunday school or with a few friends meeting in your home. "For Meditation and Discussion" questions at the end of each chapter can guide your sharing, and in sharing you can minister to one another.

Most of all, though, this book is for you personally, for times when life isn't fair to you. I know these times hurt, because life hasn't been fair to me either. When hurts do come, you and I need to be reassured. We need to know, despite everything that goes wrong, that God is Lord. And that God is good.

                                                    Larry Richards

1

Anguish
within Me

As Sue typed the letter to CAMI she could feel the pain come, as strong as it had been thirteen years ago.

"My beautiful baby girl!"

She fought back the tears, glanced at the doctor's report, and kept on typing.

It was their first child. Sue was excited as only a young woman who had dreamed of motherhood long before she was a teenager could be. She wanted to go home to have the child. But Bob scoffed. The army hospital in Germany was good enough for their friends. It was good enough for Sue, too.

So Sue worked to prepare the baby's room in their little apartment "economy" style. She painted, papered, picked out a bassinette and baby bed, sewed sets of baby clothes, and even knitted a little pink blanket. She even dreamed the little girl-to-be's name: Jennifer.

When the pain came, she and Bob hurried to the hospital. It was several hours before Sue realized something must be wrong. Finally, after twenty-four hours, they told her. The baby was breech. In the States a breech was always taken by Caesarean. One army doctor told her he'd do a Caesarean, but he was going off duty in ten minutes. It was up to the duty doctor to decide.

From that point Sue's story is a tale of horror. When she asked for a Caesarean section, the doctor coldly told her she'd just have to suffer. He then proceeded to botch the delivery in half a dozen ways, errors pointed out later by obstetricians who read the medical report and talked with Sue. For Sue's baby the story ended with her head trapped inside Sue's body, her tiny heart struggling to beat, and the doctor frantically trying to free her frail frame.

The story has never ended for Sue.

For years whenever she saw a little girl about the age Jennifer would have been—getting on a school bus, walking hand in hand with her mother, or laughing with friends—Sue felt her heart stop. Each July, when Jennifer's birthday—and death-day—arrives, Sue feels the aching loss again.

It has never ended for Sue. It never will.

"My beautiful little girl."

What hurts so much after all these years is that it was all so unnecessary. If only Bob had let her go home to have the baby. If only the other doctor had been on duty. If only the doctor who told her to "suffer" hadn't wanted to practice delivering a breech birth. *If only.* . . . Jennifer's death had not been necessary. And it just wasn't fair.

Fair Is Fair

It doesn't take a traumatic experience to convince us that life isn't fair. We learn that at a very early age.

It's our parents who teach us about fairness. "Momma!" the three-year-old howls. "She took my doll!" Momma comes and tries to help. "That belongs to Karen," Mom explains. Or maybe she asks, "Who had it first?" Or maybe Momma uses her kitchen timer. "Karen, you play with the doll for ten minutes. When the timer rings, it will be Dana's turn." Parents try so hard to develop that sense of fairness.

Of course, soon our children turn their sense of fairness against us. Ask any youngster what's not fair, and most of the things on his list will be things parents make him do!

When I asked eight-year-old Sarah for her "not fair" list, she wrote: "When they make me by [sic] things with my own money. Making me go to bed at 8:00. Not getting a phone of my own."

A soon-to-be-fourteen-year-old, Gina Norwood, gave me this list: "Bed time. Grounding. Parents. Doing dishes. Feeding animals."

Look the lists over, and you quickly sense the young person's definition of fair. "Fair" is doing what I want to do. "Not fair" is when someone keeps me from doing what I want to do, or from having what I want to have.

Actually, that's not such a terrible definition. Most of us feel the unfairness of life most intensely when we are its victim. Paul, a forty-year-old friend of mine, felt the unfairness when the IRS claimed he owed the government a large debt. Without any court proceedings the IRS simply attached his bank account. By the time Paul found out, dozens of his checks had bounced, and his credit and reputation were in shambles. Much later, after months of frustrating meetings, the IRS admitted it had been wrong. Paul was told that his money would be returned—in a few months when the papers were processed. In the meantime Paul did not receive so much as a "we're sorry."

I have times when I feel life is unfair. I felt that way nearly thirty years ago when my daughter Joy was born with brain damage. Joy now leads a relatively happy life in a fine Christian residential care community, and I'm glad for her. But when I sat this past weekend to figure my income taxes, the total of Joy's and the rest of the family's medical expenses for 1988 was $28,197.38!

I've never begrudged Joy the money. I've been grateful the Lord has provided enough so I can see Joy is cared for in a healthy, happy environment. But I have to admit that there are times I feel it just isn't fair.

What about Sue's list? Life wasn't fair when Jennifer was taken from her through the incompetence of an army doctor. How else is life unfair? Here's a list Sue gave me when I asked:

1. It's not fair when you grow up with alcoholic parents.
2. It's not fair when your sister can eat anything and you gain weight walking past a bakery.
3. It's not fair when your spouse has a middle age crisis at thirty-one and walks out on you and two babies.
4. It's not fair when your parents discourage your dreams.
5. It's not fair when you're abused and grow up with negative self-esteem.
6. It's not fair when you grow up with a physical handicap.

Margret, a teacher Sue's come to know in the high school where she teaches, could give us a lengthy list.

Some years ago Margret slipped on a piece of fruit discarded in a school hallway and injured her back. She's gone through years of operations, but still experiences intense pain. Years ago her husband decided he couldn't stand living with a cripple, and he deserted her. This year, after another operation that again failed to help, Margret has been forced into early retirement from teaching. She has pain when she stands. When she walks. When she lies down. And now she can't even look forward to coming to work to take her mind off her loneliness.

It's not just that our parents teach us fair is fair. Somehow we all intuitively sense that by rights everything ought to be fair. So it's especially hard when life isn't fair to us. The "not fair" lists we make change as we grow older. But the feelings children and adults experience may be much the same.

We're hurt.

We're frightened.

At times we're angry.

We feel vulnerable and alone.

David the psalmist picks up those feelings in Psalm 55. David has been praying, but somehow God seems to have ignored David's plea. Disturbed by his troubles and by his own thoughts, David says to God:

> My heart is in anguish within me;
>   the terrors of death assail me.
> Fear and trembling have beset me;
>   horror has overwhelmed me.
> I said, "Oh, that I had the wings of a dove!
>   I would fly away and be at rest—
> I would flee far away,
>   and stay in the desert;

> I would hurry to my place of shelter,
>   far from tempest and storm."
>
> Psalm 55:4–8

But when life isn't fair, there's no place to flee. We have to stay. Even when our hearts are in anguish.

Life, Fair?

What bothers some isn't just the pain, but being forced to face the fact that life isn't fair. The basic moral principle that mom and dad tried to teach us—to be fair—is violated constantly in this world, in our own experience, and in the experience of people we know. No wonder one Yiddish saying goes, "If God lived on earth, people would break all his windows."

Sometimes believers insist that God *is* fair. Job, the Old Testament sufferer, got into a heated argument with three pious friends who, to "protect" God, kept on insisting that Job's troubles must be due to some hidden sin. Finally the frustrated Job challenged them with this angry outburst:

> Listen. Listen, and then mock. But now listen, and be surprised.
>
> You talk about the end of the wicked. Well, look around. We each know wicked men who do prosper. They get old. They see their grandchildren. Their houses are safe; nothing bad seems to happen to them.
>
> God doesn't use his rod on them. Why, they even mock God. They say, "Why serve God? We're doing all right without him. Where's the profit in prayer?"
>
> How often do folks like this really get what they deserve?

"Oh," you say, "they get it in the end."
But *when?* Why, God's children seem to suffer more
than the ungodly!
Who repays the wicked? Your answers are all lies!

Job 21:1–34
[author's paraphrase]

Philosophers use the realities that Job observed here
to challenge the very existence of Scripture's God. They
argue, "If God is good, he doesn't want human beings to
suffer unfairly. If God is all-powerful, he can stop such
suffering. So, since human beings do suffer unfairly, it
follows that God either is not good, or that God is not all
powerful."

Perhaps it's this that sometimes makes those comforting verses of Psalm 100 seem like empty words. The
psalmist says, "The Lord is God." He also says, "The Lord
is good." And, deep down, we sense the contradiction.

How can a good God, an all-powerful God, permit
human beings to suffer unfairly? Why do the Jennifers
die? Why are children like my Joy brain-damaged at
birth? Why are the rights of the Pauls sometimes disre-
garded by a government sworn to protect them? Why
must the Margrets face years of pain? Why is life so
often so terribly, tragically, painfully unfair?

In a delightful book, *The Joys of Yiddish,* Leo Rosten
tells the story of an old Jew who, on the eve of Yom
Kippur, the solemn Day of Atonement (when all practic-
ing Jews fast and ask forgiveness for their sins) looked up
to heaven and sighed.

"Dear God, listen. I, Hershel the tailor, put it to You!
The butcher in our village, Shepsel, is a good man, an
honorable man, who never cheats anyone, and always
gives full weight, and never turns away the needy: yet

Shepsel himself is so poor that he and his wife sometimes go without meat! . . . Or take Fishel, our shoemaker, a model of piety and kindness—yet his beloved mother is dying in terrible pain. . . . And Reb Label, our *melamed* (teacher), who loves all the lads he teaches and is loved by all who know him—lives hand to mouth, hasn't a decent suit to his name, and just developed an eye disease that may leave him blind! . . . So, on this most holy night, I ask You directly, God: Is this *fair?* I repeat: *Is this fair?* . . . So, tomorrow, O Lord, on our sacred Yom Kippur—if You forgive us, we will forgive You!"

Forgiven, or Understood?

Sometimes we may very well feel that God needs forgiveness for permitting the things we experience or read about. The papers here in Florida last year were full of stories about the Olympic diver whose car smashed into a group of teens so violently that some of their bodies were literally torn apart. At the last moment he pled guilty of manslaughter. He was driving at seventy miles an hour, and the alcohol content in his blood was twice Florida's legal standard of drunkenness.

Not long ago another drunk driver smashed into the side of a church bus in Kentucky. Because a bus company tried to save a few extra pennies, a safety cage had not been bolted around the gas tank. The gas tank exploded, and twenty-seven young people were burned to death.

Few Christians would have the boldness of Hershel the tailor to offer God forgiveness. Many Christians feel the pain of the parents in the two accidents, offer a prayer, and try to forget we live in a world that is so terribly unfair. When challenged, we Christians tend either to offer the opinion that "it was all in God's plan," or perhaps to insist that "God had nothing to do with it."

The tragedy is that neither answer satisfies. And neither answer faces the moral challenge that life's unfairness poses. The twin affirmation, "The Lord is God," and "the Lord is good," truly is called into question by the unfairness of life.

But what we need is not to forgive God.

What we really need is to understand God's goodness. And, in understanding the goodness of God, to know inner peace when life isn't fair, and "anguish is within me."

There are three things you can do, even before you read on, to begin to understand the goodness of God.

(1) *Don't try to protect God by refusing to face reality.* God doesn't need our protection. He can take care of himself, and guard his own glory. Most of all, God doesn't need us to lie for him. Life really is not fair. Terrible things do happen. The sin of Job's three friends was that in trying to protect God from Job's charge of unfairness they did not "speak of me [God] what is right, as my servant Job has" (Job 42:7). Job faced the fact of life's unfairness, and struggled to understand. His friends tried to deny that reality. So begin your quest to understand God's goodness by acknowledging the fact that many things that happen to good people are completely unfair. Things that have happened to *you* are unfair. You can't please God by candy-coating this reality, or pretending that nothing has ever been wrong.

(2) *Don't expect to find totally satisfying answers.* God doesn't mind us questioning him. In fact, God has opened his heart, and given us access to his thoughts, through the Scriptures. But human beings are finite and God is infinite. We are limited; he is vast beyond our capacity to grasp. Scripture cloaks in words mysteries that we will never fully understand until we are raised up to be with Christ and share his splendor.

In the meantime, the insights we come across will be enough to reassure the man or woman of faith that God truly is good. To those without faith, the answers we find may not merely be unsatisfying, they may even seem foolish.

(3) *Do give Scripture a chance to speak.* It's all too easy, when we're caught up in our own anguish or moved by the anguish of others, to hear only those cries of pain. The cries are so loud they often drown out the voice of a God who never shouts at us, yet who never stops speaking to us in quiet, loving tones.

We need to step back a bit from the experiences that make life unfair and be willing to open our hearts to God. We need to let his Word give us perspective on the pain. We need to let his Spirit give us insight, not so much into the "why," but into the "how"—how we can find healing ourselves, and how we can become agents of healing for others.

For Meditation or Discussion

1. If you were to make a "Not fair" list as Sue did, what would you include? Include those things in your own life you feel were unfair.

2. Make a list of persons who have had experiences that you think aren't fair. I mentioned Paul's experience with the IRS, and also Margret, who taught with Sue until her pain forced her to retire. How many people with experiences like theirs can you think of?

3. Read and think about Psalm 100. What verses would be especially comforting to a person in anguish over something that isn't fair? What verses do you think would be hard for such a person to "hear"?

2

Some Time
Later

You can almost hear the brothers whispering together as their father lies dying in the next room. "As soon as dad dies, the kid goes," the eldest says, glancing at the youngster huddled in the corner, his eyes downcast, not quite crying even though Gilead, the father he loves, is nearly dead.

"It won't be long now," another brother agrees. He too glances at the boy, and then says, "I'll be glad to see the last of *him*."

Of course, if you would talk to the brothers, they'd have a list of pious reasons for what they planned to do. The boy in the corner, Jephthah [Jeff-tha], was a son their father had with a prostitute. Dad had the gall to acknowledge him and bring him into the family. How that must have hurt mom! If dad felt responsible, he could have paid someone to care for the kid, and at least have kept him out of sight!

The fact is, these sons of Gilead's wife had another reason for their actions. The reason comes through loud and clear in their words as they drove Jephthah away. "You are not going to get any inheritance in our family."

Apparently it wasn't hard to get the legal backing

necessary to disinherit the young half-brother. Gilead's sons went to the leaders of the community, stated their case, and were given full cooperation. The Bible passage that relates the story says the brothers "drove" their half-brother away, and that he "fled from his brothers." Jephthah's rejection was complete. He lost his father. He was driven from the familiar surroundings in which he'd begun to grow up. And every person he'd known in his whole life seemed to turn against him.

Of all the things in life that aren't fair, a child's rejection by adults may be the most painful. Perhaps grown-ups can handle such pain. But why must terrible things happen to children?

Something like this happened to Ray Charles, the popular musician who was born into desperate poverty. He began to go blind at age 5—and was left alone in a state institution as a teenager when his parents died.

I read about Ray Charles in an interview carried in *Parade* magazine on August 7, 1988. Here's Ray's story in his own words:

"We were in a very small town and very poor, and there were no such things as psychologists to teach my mom how to raise a kid who was an oddity in that town. I was the only blind kid in this little town, so that made me odd to all the other kids. You know, people laugh a little. They don't know. But my mom, she somehow knew that there's nothing wrong with my brain. I just couldn't see.

"She made me do everything other kids did. I mean, I had to make my bed. I had to scrub the floor and wash the dishes. My mom taught me how to cook. It was mirac-ulous, this woman, to me. Can you imagine an extremely poor family in the South where, if we didn't raise our own vegetables, I'm sure we would have starved to death? Me and my mom had a little garden out back. You see, when she knew I was going to lose my sight, she knew she had to teach me how to do normal things, to learn so I could take care of myself when she was gone."

At the age of seven Ray was sent to a state institution for the blind. That year his right eye began to pain him so intensely that it had to be removed.

"The kids come from all over the state," Ray remembers, "and go to the school to live. If you went home—say, Christmastime or Easter—your parents had to pay for the ticket home. I had my parents until I was 15, but we didn't have the money, so I missed going home for the holidays. I had to stay at school, which was a hurtin' feeling. You feel bad, you hurt about something when it's happening to you at the moment, but after that you manage to get over it. The whole school was nearly empty except for a few of us kids who couldn't afford to go home. I had this little thing—I like music—and that was one time I could get in the piano room without having any trouble. This campus I'm speaking of had what they called the colored side and the white side. The only time you went on the, quote, 'white side' was if you got sick, because that's where the hospital was. Now this was a *blind* school. Stupid, isn't it? The piano room was on the white side, and I liked playing the piano, but I couldn't always use it—except on the holidays when everybody was gone. So it worked out a little bit."

It Worked Out a Little Bit

We don't have a report of any interviews given by Jephthah. But we do have two chapters of the book of Judges devoted to his story (chapters 11–12).

Jephthah grew up at a time when the Israelites had abandoned God for the pagan deities of the surrounding nations. Because of this sin God permitted the Israelites to be oppressed by the Philistines in the west, and the Amorites in the east. Perhaps the spiritual decline of those days helps explain the brutal way in which Jephthah was treated by his brothers and his community.

At any rate, Jephthah, now settled in an area called Tob, grew up to be as skilled in warfare as Ray Charles is in music. As Jephthah's reputation grew, so did the number of his followers. Then, "some time later," the Ammonites decided to mount a major attack and take over the entire area east of the Jordan that was occupied by Israel. Frantic, the elders of Gilead, who years earlier had stood by and watched Jephthah driven away, came to see the now mature warrior.

The scene is rich in irony. Here's how Judges 11: 6–11, describes it.

> "Come," the elders said to Jephthah, "be our commander, so we can fight the Ammonites."
>
> Jephthah said to them, "Didn't you hate me, and drive me from my father's house? Why do you come to me now, when you're in trouble?"
>
> The elders of Gilead said to him, "Nevertheless, we are turning to you now; come with us to fight the Ammonites, and you will be our head over all who live in Gilead."
>
> Jephthah answered, "Suppose you take me back to fight the Ammonites and the Lord gives them to me— will I really be your head?"
>
> The elders of Gilead replied, "The Lord is our witness; we will certainly do as you say." So Jephthah went with the elders of Gilead, and the people made him head and commander over them. And he repeated all his words before the Lord in Mizpah.

What stuns us, however, is to read the letter that Jephthah sent to the Ammonite king. In that letter Jephthah displays a thorough knowledge of Israel's history, and a deep faith in God! Jephthah concludes his letter by saying, "Let the Lord, the Judge, decide the dispute this day between the Israelites and the Ammonites" (v. 27).

Somehow Jephthah, the child who was rejected by his family and by the community of Israel, maintained a personal commitment to God, and now displayed a courageous faith in the Lord, the God of the people who had driven him out!

It's strange, isn't it?

The sons Gilead had by his wife showed none of the compassion that marks a true faith in God. It's the son of the prostitute—Jephthah, the boy who was rejected and suffered so much anguish in childhood—who searched for and who found spiritual reality.

Something like this happened in Ray Charles' life. The interviewer asked Ray, "One of the great questions in life goes back to Job: 'Why do good men suffer?' You're a good man, yet you're blind. You lost your parents. You suffered bigotry and rough times. And yet there seems to be no bitterness, no anger. Why is that?"

Ray replied, "That's a nice point in talking about Job. If you want to say, as a kid who comes up from a very, very poverty-stricken area, where he goes around with holes in his pants and little patches on his clothes and barefoot and all, and yet sat down in the presence of three Presidents of the most powerful country in the world—I mean, there are people who live forever and don't get to do that! You understand what I'm saying?

I've had tragedies in my life, you know, but you got to tell yourself, if you believe in the good, what Job knew in the end: 'The Lord giveth and the Lord taketh away.' And you've got to remember that 'taketh away' part. There's nothing written in the Bible, in the Old or New Testament, where it says: 'If you believe in Me, you ain't going to have no trouble.' As a matter of fact, if you look at most of the people who were followers of God, they had all kinds of problems. Although I've had bad things happen to me—let's face it, let's be honest about it— would you say I'm probably better off than most sighted people?

"I think I'm a contented man. I'm blessed that I'm able to say that to you. I've learned, number one, how to let things that don't mean a thing go by me. I mean that sincerely, I've learned to appreciate when people are kind to me. I have no regrets, and I thank God for that.

"I would just like to work with people with talent. And I guess the last thing, hopefully, is to continue to play my music, sing my songs and make the public happy. If I could just do that until the Good Lord says, 'Okay, I'm going to rein you in,' that'd be cool for me."

Jephthah won his battle with the Ammonites. He led his army, "and the Lord gave them into his hand." But the victory was a costly one for Jephthah personally.

In Old Testament times any Israelite might make a voluntary vow to the Lord. In this vow a person pledged to make a particular sacrifice or give certain property as an offering to God. Vows were generally made either as an act of faith, pledging a gift to be given when a prayer was answered, or an act of gratitude, a thank offering given for some unexpected blessing. Before the battle but after the Spirit of the Lord had come upon him (11:29), Jephthah made a vow to sacrifice as a burnt offering "whatever comes out of the door of my house to meet me when I return in triumph from the Ammonites" (11:31).

The Israelites east of the Jordan kept large flocks and herds. In those days the lower level of two-story houses were typically occupied by farm animals. Probably Jephthah expected one of these farm animals—a sheep, a cow, or a goat—to be the first out the door after he returned. But when Jephthah did return victorious, it was his daughter—Jephthah's only child—who hurried out of the house to greet him!

Jewish and Christian commentators have debated whether Jephthah actually offered his daughter as a human sacrifice. But lines of Bible teaching suggest he did not. First, human sacrifice is forbidden in God's law (Leviticus 18:21; 20:2–5; Deuteronomy 12:31; 18:10). Jephthah's familiarity with biblical history indicates he would have understood this fact, and never violated such a clear prohibition. Second, no priest would have officiated at such a rite, and only a descendant of Aaron was qualified to officiate at a sacrifice. Third, the law concerning vows offers an alternative. A person dedicated to the Lord could fulfill his or her parents' vow by lifelong service rather than death. Fourth, the text itself says that Jephthah's daughter asked for time to weep "because I will never be married" (Judges 11:37). She clearly was not looking forward to death, but to a celibate life dedicated to serving God.

For Jephthah even this was a tragedy. Why? Because as Jephthah's only child, his daughter might have married, and her first son would be given her father's name, inherit his property, and carry on the family line. With his daughter committed to God, Jephthah knew his line would die out with him.

Jephthah lived for only six more years. During that time he served as Judge (leader) of the Israelites who lived in Gilead. But Jephthah's fame lived on. Centuries later the writer of the New Testament book of Hebrews listed Jephthah among the heroes who, by faith, "administered justice, and gained what was promised" (Hebrews 11:32, 33).

Ray Charles has gained fame too—honors that, as he says, "you don't normally get unless you're very ancient or you're dead." Among those honors are many Grammys, the Grammy Lifetime Achievement Award, two Emmys, and Kennedy Center recognition. Most important, perhaps, are the songs this 58-year-old blind composer has recorded, including "America the Beautiful" and the official song of the state of Georgia, "Georgia on My Mind."

Yet I'm sure that if you or I had seen Jephthah, a mere youngster being driven from his home by his jeering half-brothers, our hearts would have gone out to him. And we would have cried, "It's not fair!"

If you or I had seen Ray Charles, a blind and ragged black child, if we'd seen the discrimination he experienced in the institution where he grew up, or if we'd known or felt the pain caused by a poverty so deep that even a train ticket home for the holidays was beyond the family's means, we'd have wept for him. "It's not fair," we would have said.

And we would have been right.

It's only now, some time later, that we can put those early experiences in perspective. Somehow, even though life wasn't fair to Jephthah or Ray, we know today that neither one was ruined by the injustices he experienced. We can even sense that, somehow, God used those early hurts redemptively.

Somehow, Jephthah's faith was fanned into a brighter flame.

Somehow, Ray Charles found contentment, and developed a resourcefulness and enthusiasm seldom found in persons whose childhoods were what we think of as ideal.

We may not understand it. But there are just too many people who have overcome difficulties, who have been tested by adversity and strengthened by it, for us to accept the notion that what isn't fair is automatically harmful.

Perhaps, just perhaps, God actually used the terrible injustices each of these men faced to stimulate their growth. Perhaps, just perhaps, neither would have matured as a person, or developed his talent, without that early pain.

That's not to imply that the unfair things which happen to us are "good." But it does imply that we should not hastily identify the unfair as "bad" either.

Sometimes even nature works this way. The only way to strengthen a muscle is to use it. In the process, muscle tissue is first broken down, and only then replaced with stronger, thicker fibers. Muscle builders have a saying, "No pain, no gain." Unless you're willing to stand the pain that comes with heavy workouts, your muscles will not grow but remain weak.

Perhaps, just perhaps, the unfair things we experience in life are designed for our spiritual rather than physical development. Perhaps only by stretching us, by challenging us with heavier and heavier weights, can God make us truly strong.

What do we learn in comparing the lives of Jephthah and of our contemporary, Ray Charles?

(1) *We learn to be more sensitive to pain.* It may well be that God uses the hurts we experience to strengthen us. It may well be that the character as well as the talents of persons like Jephthah and Ray Charles are honed by childhood pain. But one thing is sure. The anguish each of these two men experienced was very real. Whatever redemptive use God had in mind for that pain, you and I must be willing to feel it.

We must be sensitive to loneliness, aware of the fears. We must be willing to take those who hurt in our arms, and let them know that someone cares.

There may be very little we can do to change this world. We can hardly rid it of injustice, nor can we take every hurting child into our home. But whatever we can do to express love and compassion, that we should do. And do soon.

(2) *We learn that life is never void of hope.* It was during a time of national disaster that the prophet Jeremiah spoke these words to a frightened and discouraged people: "I know the plans I have for you," declares the Lord, "plans to prosper you and not to harm you, plans to give you hope and a future" (Jeremiah 29:11).

If we look at any person's life while he or she is experiencing some serious injustice, present pain is likely to distort our perspective. Only time can give us perspective. Only some time later can we begin to tell what positive values the unfair things we experience may have.

The believer maintains perspective by looking beyond the present—and by realizing that God does care. God, who cares, speaks to us in our present pain and reassures us. His plans cannot be thwarted even by what is unfair. And he does not intend to harm us. He gives us hope—and a future.

(3) *God is available when life is unfair.* It's fascinating, but the tragedies represented in the early lives of Jephthah and Ray Charles did not alienate either one from God. In fact, I suspect the pain made them even more sensitive to him. Somehow when you and I suffer we become intensely aware that we can't make it alone. That life holds challenges we can't meet on our own.

When that realization comes, a single glance in his direction makes us aware of God. In our need, we reach out. In reaching out, we find him. And in finding God, we find the resource we need to survive when life is unfair.

For Meditation and Discussion

1. Read Judges 11–13 carefully. How many things beside Jephthah's rejection by his family and community can you sense that might have been on his "not fair" list?

2. From the picture of the adult Jephthah drawn in these Judges chapters, what kind of person do you think he became? List characteristics or qualities suggested by the biblical text. Do you think any are related to the unfair things he experienced when young? Which ones, and how might they be related?

3. Think back over some of the things on the "not fair" list you made for yourself. Now that it is some time later in your life, can you see any positive contributions those experiences may have made to you?

4. The author suggests that God may be very close when life isn't fair. How have you experienced God at such times?

3

Who Will Show
Us Any Good?

King David, in one of two psalms that reflect on his experience when he was driven from Jerusalem by his own son, Absalom, penned the words in the title of this chapter. "Many are asking," David wrote, "'Who will show us any good?'" (Psalm 4:6).

It's a good question. A question anyone might ask when he or she is living through one of those troubled times when life isn't fair.

But there's a problem with that question. "Good" is such a slippery term. We use it so many different ways. Webster's *New World Dictionary* lists seventeen different major meanings within its general sense of approval or commendation! According to Webster, "good" can mean:

> 1. a) suitable to a purpose; effective; efficient b) producing favorable results; beneficial 2. fertile 3. fresh; unspoiled; uncontaminated 4. valid; genuine; real 5. healthy; strong; vigorous 6. financially safe or sound 7. honorable; worthy; respectable 8. enjoyable, desirable, pleasant, happy 9. dependable; reliable; right 10. thorough; complete 11. excellent of its kind 12. best, or considered satisfying 13. morally sound or excellent; specif., a) virtuous; honest; just b) pious;

31

devout c) kind, benevolent, generous, sympathetic d) well behaved; dutiful 14. proper, becoming; correct 15. able; skilled; expert 16. loyal or conforming 17. *Law* effectual; valid.

The dictionary goes on to give even more definitions under "good's" intensive meaning—a good many, a morally good man, etc.

The fact that good has so many different shades of meaning raises a question about that argument philosophers use against God. Remember it? If God were good and all powerful, they say, he wouldn't let unfair things happen to people. The argument hinges on the notion that, whatever the unfair experiences of our life may be, they surely can never be classified—in any sense—as "good."

But it's obvious that many of the unfair things which happen to us *can* be called good within this word's definition!

Last weekend my wife Sue was taking a course, Teacher Effectiveness Training, in Orlando. It's one of those things teachers do—keep on taking college courses not just to maintain their accreditation but also because many are dedicated to doing a really good job in the classroom.

During the weekend one of the exercises called for each teacher to share something about herself—something personal and significant. Sue shared a few of the things on that "not fair" list I included in the first chapter.

It wasn't fair for her to grow up in a home with two alcoholic parents. It wasn't fair for her husband of eight years to leave her with a two-and-a-half-year-old boy when she was three months pregnant. It wasn't fair to have to struggle to care for the two children, maintain a home, take classes to get her teaching certificate, all the while suffering from exhaustion and arthritis. But, as part of her sharing, Sue said, "I know that while it wasn't easy, the Lord used it to make me a better person."

As the group later gave her and the others feedback, they agreed. "I can see how you developed strength." "I like the way you've kept your sense of humor." "I really admire your courage."

No one would want to live through the pain Sue experienced in those days when life was so unfair. But Sue herself, and others, can look at her now and honestly say that those experiences were beneficial. They helped her grow into the person she has become. And remember: within the dictionary definition, what is beneficial is, ultimately, "good."

David, who knew intense pain when his son led a rebellion against him, understood this truth. "It was good for me to be afflicted," David wrote in Psalm 119:71, "so that I might learn your decrees."

Oh, yes. It hurt. It was unfair. But through his affliction, David learned more about the Lord.

Deceptively Simple

That word "good" is deceptively simple. When we use it, we think we know just what we mean. But often we haven't thought it through.

In the Hebrew Old Testament the word commonly translated "good" is *tob*. It means good in the broadest possible sense. The good is the beautiful, the attractive, the useful, the profitable, the desirable, the morally right.

What links all these meanings, says the *Expository Dictionary of Bible Words*, is evaluation. "To determine the good, one must compare things, qualities, and actions with other qualities, things, and actions. One must contrast the beneficial and the right with other things that are not beneficial and are wrong.

"Because God shared his image and likeness with mankind, human beings have the capacity to make value judgments. But sin has distorted humanity's perceptions. Because of this, only God is able to evaluate perfectly. The writers of the OT were convinced that not only was God the giver and the measure of good but also that he alone knows what is truly beneficial for us and what is morally right" (p. 316).

What a challenge for faith—really to believe that God alone knows what is beneficial for us, as well as what is morally right!

And to face the unfair things which happen to us with the confidence that, somehow, God means them for our good!

Another of David's psalms admits that "a righteous man may have many troubles." But it then goes on to affirm that "the Lord delivers him from them all." In the ongoing cycle of troubles and deliverance that marks all our lives, David is sure of this: "those who seek the Lord lack no good thing."

Oh, perhaps from our human viewpoint we lack many things that we consider good. But from God's viewpoint, where the "good" is primarily the beneficial rather than the pleasant, we are richly supplied. Look at the words of this psalm. Think what the words meant to a troubled David. And what the words mean to you.

This poor man called, and the Lord heard him;
he saved him out of all his troubles.
The angel of the Lord encamps around those who fear him,
and he delivers them.

Taste and see that the Lord is good;
blessed is the man who takes refuge in him.
Fear the Lord, you his saints,
for those who fear him lack nothing.
The lions may grow weak and hungry,
but those who seek the Lord lack no good thing.

Come, my children, listen to me;
I will teach you the fear of the Lord.
Whoever of you loves life
and desires to see many good days,
keep your tongue from evil
and your lips from speaking lies.
Turn from evil and do good;
seek peace and pursue it.

The eyes of the Lord are on the righteous
and his ears are open to their cry;
the face of the Lord is against those who do evil,
to cut off the memory of them from the earth.

The righteous cry out, and the Lord hears them;
he delivers them from all their troubles.
The Lord is close to the brokenhearted
and saves those who are crushed in spirit.

A righteous man may have many troubles,
but the Lord delivers him from them all;
he protects all his bones,
not one of them will be broken.

Evil will slay the wicked;
   the foes of the righteous will be condemned.
The Lord redeems his servants;
   no one who takes refuge in him will be condemned.

Psalm 34:6–22

For Your Comfort and Salvation

As Sue typed the letter to CAMI she could feel the pain come, as strong as it had been thirteen years ago.

"My beautiful baby girl!"

She fought back the tears, glanced at the doctor's report, and kept on typing.

Sue doesn't like to relive those terrible days in the Army hospital in Germany when Jennifer was taken from her so unfairly. But she felt she had to write her letter, even though it brought back such vivid memories.

CAMI stands for Concerned Americans for Military Improvements. It's an organization typified by Mary Day, whose nineteen-year-old son died in a Navy hospital in 1978. After a lengthy struggle to uncover the facts, Mrs. Day established, despite denials by the Navy, that her son was killed by a serious heart condition which went undiagnosed by military doctors. Somehow, despite his weight loss of some 48 pounds, the Navy doctors decided Chuck Day's problems were "all in his head." It was not until the day before Chuck died that the Navy scheduled tests that, according to Dr. William Q. Sturner, chief medical examiner for the state of Rhode Island, could have diagnosed his disease and saved his life.

Mary Day was determined that her Chuck must not have died in vain. And so she began her fight for improvements in the military health system. *There's nothing I can do for my son*, Mary Day thought, *but there's a lot of other mothers' sons out there and it's not going to happen to them.*

She began a barrage of badgering letters to Navy officials, congressmen, and senators. Then in 1982 Mrs. Day watched a Phil Donahue TV show featuring parents from around the country whose children had also died under suspicious circumstances while serving in the peacetime military.

It was then she learned about CAMI, a group that today has some 1,600 members in twenty-six states. For the last seven years Mrs. Day and other CAMI members have met in Washington for an annual national convention and to lobby Congress. CAMI members regularly testify before important congressional committees. Largely through CAMI's efforts, significant changes have been made in military medical care.*

Among the letters telling of inadequate medical care that has influenced Congress and the Pentagon was Sue's. It hurt to write the letter. It hurt to remember— and feel again—the injustice and the loss. And there is really no way that you or I could argue that the loss of Sue's baby was beneficial to her. But Sue, like others in CAMI, are determined that their loss will benefit others.

Next week Sue starts a new class in her local Methodist Church. The class is a continuation of a four-week

* For further information on CAMI, contact Joan or Joseph Connors, Ocala, FL (904) 237-1690.

introduction she taught on "Growing through Divorce." The class demonstrates again how the unfair things that happen to us can benefit others.

It was devastating to Sue when her husband left. She hadn't expected it. After all, she was just three months pregnant! But Sue knew she had to deal with this experience as with everything in life. So Sue enrolled in an eight-week series of seminars on divorce offered in her hometown. She became active in the group, and soon was serving as an area coordinator and facilitator for the seminars. She was instrumental in starting a class for singles in her local church, and soon was hosting a single's Bible study in her home.

Later Sue wrote a book, *Effective Divorce Ministry* (Zondervan, 1986), to help leaders in local churches understand what happens inside a person going through a divorce, and how to structure various kinds of programs to minister to them. Sue has ministered to many struggling with the pain of divorce in conferences, and taught Sunday school electives in the local churches she has attended.

Was Sue's experience of desertion and divorce "good"? Never! Not in the sense of desirable or pleasant. The divorce was a tragedy, an injustice. The divorce was something everyone would include on a list of things in life that just plain aren't fair. Yet perhaps in a broader perspective, Sue's experience *was* "good." In a peculiar way it was beneficial for her—through her pain Sue grew spiritually and as a person. And, in a peculiar way, it was beneficial for others. Because Sue was hurt, she has been able to minister to many, many others who are hurting too.

In 2 Corinthians 1 the apostle Paul, who knew pain and anguish well, expresses his praise "to the God and Father of our Lord Jesus Christ, the Father of compassion and the God of all comfort." Paul goes on to explain that God comforts us "in all our troubles, so that we can comfort those in any trouble with the comfort we ourselves have received from God" (vv. 3, 4).

It is a simple but vital principle of Christian life. The thing that qualifies you or me to comfort others is our pain. Only when we suffer are we able to identify with those who suffer. Only when we've turned to God, and experienced the comfort he gives us, are we enabled to comfort them. And so, Paul writes, "if we are distressed, it is for your comfort and salvation."

No wonder we need to leave the evaluation of what is "good" up to the Lord!

If you or I were to choose our own path in life, we'd carefully avoid all those things that seem so unfair. We'd never choose the loss of child. We'd never choose the destruction of a marriage. Surely, in the sense of pleasant or enjoyable, such experiences are not "good."

But perhaps, just perhaps, in a larger sense of "good," the pain we experience may benefit us—and others!

How can we discover the good hidden within the unfair things that happen to us? Here are a few thoughts that may help.

(1) *Examine the personal qualities unfair experiences call forth.* Any unfair experience forces us to exercise special qualities. James goes so far as to say, "consider it pure joy" when you face various trials. Such experiences

demand perseverance, and "perseverance must finish its work so that you may be mature and complete" (James 1:2–4). Paul makes a similar observation. "We rejoice in our sufferings," he writes in Romans, "because we know that suffering produces perseverance; perseverance, character; and character, hope" (Romans 5:3, 4).

So when life isn't fair it's wise to stop and think about the particular quality of character we need to exercise in order to persevere. Scripture provides several good checklists. Three are found in Galatians 5:22, 23, Romans 12:9–21, and 1 Corinthians 13:4–7.

The two Greek words translated "good" in the New Testament are *agathos* and *kalos*. While they are treated as synonyms, there are shades of difference. What makes *kalos* special is that it emphasizes the aesthetic aspect of goodness. The good is not just beneficial, it is beautiful. It's this we discover as we live through life's unfair experiences and suddenly realize that God has used them to build distinctive Christian qualities into our lives. God is not only making us righteous. Through many of the unfair things in life, God is making us beautiful.

(2) *Explore the opportunities to minister that an unfair experience creates.* I remember leaning over a back fence in Illinois, being introduced to the relative of a neighbor. As we talked in that stiffly formal way strangers have, my daughter Joy came up. The eyes of the stranger lit up, and she said, "We have a retarded child, too!" In a moment of time a bond of common experience was created, and we were no longer strangers.

The *other* Greek word translated "good," *agathos*, has the special meaning of useful, or beneficial. When something unfair happens to you, look around. Are there others who have had a similar experience? God may use the pain to create a bond between you—a bond that will enable you to share the comfort with which the Lord has comforted you.

(3) *Expect the experience to draw you closer to God.* This thought underlies Psalm 34. "This poor man called, and the Lord heard him, and saved him out of all his troubles. . . . Taste and see that the Lord is good. . . . The righteous cry out, and the Lord hears them; he delivers them from all their troubles. . . . The Lord is close to the broken hearted. . . . A righteous man may have many troubles, but the Lord delivers him from them all."

What a comfort.

God does use those unfair experiences that cause us so much pain. But God doesn't make us live through them alone! He is with us through it all, near enough to hear us when we cry out. Near enough for us to taste and see, even through the pain, that he is good. Near enough to deliver us from anything that would harm us.

For Meditation and Discussion

1. People who suffer because of life's unfairness often cry out, "Who can show us any good?" What do you feel is the most satisfying answer you might give such persons?

2. What definitions of "good" does the author suggest we consider when thinking about life's unfairness? What definitions of "good" do you think he would reject?

3. Look up the qualities listed in Galatians 5:22, 23; Romans 12:9–21; and 1 Corinthians 13:4–7. Think back over the "not fair" list you made after reading chapter 1. Which of these qualities are associated with the experiences you jotted down then?

4. Choose at least two verses of Psalm 34 to memorize. Share the verses with one other person, and tell why you selected those verses.

4

I Am
Generous

Recently our Florida state lotto game had a jackpot that attracted nationwide attention. Fifty-five million dollars—all, as the lotto advertising says, "to a single winner!"

Our local papers were filled with it too. *The St. Petersburg Times* carried one long article by a professional financial adviser, suggesting how the winner should handle all that money. The advisor suggested, first of all, that the winner try to live on just $300,000 of the $2,750,000 he or she would take home each of the next twenty years. He then went on to show in detail just how to invest the rest—in Florida beach property, in stocks, bonds, various funds, and so on. By the time he was done, 100 percent of the unused winnings had been distributed to investments that would multiply the 55 million to hundreds of millions.

That advisor was playing a familiar game. It's an old game, one that has been played as long as human beings have been on earth. It's the game of gain, and the person with the most toys when he or she dies—whether stocks, bonds, houses, jewels, cars, or big bills—wins!

It's fascinating how many of Jesus' parables concern money. Actually, ten of Christ's thirty major parables feature it. Many of them are familiar. There's the story of the lost coin (Luke 15:8–10); the story of the unjust steward—these days called the story of the "shrewd manager" (Luke 16:1–15). Then there's the parable of the unmerciful servant (Matthew 18:21–35), the parable of workers in the vineyard (Matthew 20:1–16), and, of course, the familiar parable of the rich fool (Luke 12:16–21).

There is, of course, a reason why so many of Jesus' stories and so much of his teaching deal with money. In the first century, like today, riches were symbolic of blessing. When the poor or middle class person says "life isn't fair," what he or she often means is, "Some people have lots of money and I don't."

Life isn't fair. Some people can take cruises, but I have to stay home when I take off work. Some people drive a Mercedes. I have a beat-up Chevy. Some people own their own home, giant screen TV's, and swimming pools. I have to scrape to pay the rent on this two-bit apartment, and my TV's an old 21" color portable. Some people eat out at fine restaurants. I get to stop at McDonald's. Some people wear tailored suits and designer dresses. I shop at K-Mart.

When we look at the wide spectrum of economic resources people have, we're forced to admit it: Life *isn't* fair. Some have more than enough. Some barely scrape by. What's worse, many who have didn't even earn it— they inherited it. Or they were born into a family whose cultural advantages permitted them to go to good schools, get a college education, and then slip easily into a high paying job.

No, there are such vast differences between the circumstances of people, even people in our blessed land, that we have to admit it. Life isn't fair.

When Is a Blessing a Curse?

The attitude of those who listened to Jesus teach two thousand years ago was shaped by one of two lines of teaching about money found in the Old Testament.

That line of teaching portrays wealth as a blessing which God promised to give to those Israelites who obeyed his law. This promise wasn't lightly given. It was part of the contract, or Covenant, formally drawn up between God and the people of Israel, and was carefully defined in the Law of Moses. The book of Deuteronomy contains many expressions of the divine contract.

> If you pay attention to these laws and are careful to follow them, then the Lord your God will keep his covenant of love with you, as he swore to your forefathers. He will love you and bless you and increase your numbers. He will bless the fruit of your womb, the crops of your land—your grain, new wine and oil—the calves in your herds and the lambs of your flocks in the land he swore to your forefathers to give you. You will be blessed more than any other people; none of your men or women will be childless, nor any of your livestock without young (7:12–14).

And again,

> The Lord your God is bringing you into a good land—a land with streams and pools of water, with springs flowing in the valleys and hills; a land with wheat and barley, vines and fig trees, pomegranates, olive oil and

honey; a land where bread will not be scarce and you will lack nothing; a land where the rocks are iron and you can dig copper out of the hills (8:7–9).

These, and many other passages like them, associate prosperity with godliness. This led the Jews of Jesus' time to believe that the mere possession of wealth proved the rich man was godly! After all, God had promised to bless the obedient Jew with prosperity. If a man were prosperous, he must therefore be an obedient Jew!

We see this attitude in the reaction of Jesus' disciples to a remark Christ made. A rich young man had come to Jesus and asked what good thing he must do to be saved (Matthew 19:16–27). Jesus told him to sell all he possessed, and then follow Christ as an ordinary disciple. Faced with a choice between obedience to Jesus and his money, the young man "went away sad, because he had great wealth." When he had gone, Jesus shook his head and remarked, "I tell you the truth, it is hard for a rich man to enter the kingdom of heaven."

The disciples were stunned! To their way of thinking, the rich were far closer to God than the poor. Their very wealth proved it! The New Testament says, "when the disciples heard this, they were greatly astonished and asked, 'Who then can be saved?'"

If the wealthy, who have God's blessing now, are saved only with difficulty, how can the poor man, who obviously lacks the divine stamp of approval, ever hope for salvation?

The same kind of thinking often infects modern Christians. We hear it on Christian radio and TV. God wants his kids to be blessed! If you aren't rich—then claim the blessing of wealth by faith. When you become rich, it will confirm the fact that you have the kind of faith in Christ which really counts.

Of course, frequently the promise is associated with a plea for money. "Show God how much you trust him. Send us your money. When God sees what you've done, he'll bless you ten times over! Get rich—by giving your money to me." This is the gist of much that we hear.

One friend of mine received just such a letter from a well-known TV ministry. "Send us $70 dollars today, and the Lord will repay you $700 dollars within a year," the letter said. My friend wrote back. "I'm moved by your urgent need for funds. So just send me the $70. You obviously need the $700 the Lord will repay more than I do."

The shock of Jesus' disciples, and the promise made to modern Christians by some preachers, is based on the belief that wealth is "good," an unmixed blessing from God. The problem with this view is that it ignores the other line of teaching on wealth woven through the Old Testament and reflected in Jesus' parables.

The same Deuteronomy passage that promises wealth to obedient Israelites goes on to add this warning:

> When you have eaten and are satisfied, praise the Lord your God for the good land he has given you. Be careful that you do not forget the Lord your God, failing to observe his commands, his laws and his decrees that I am giving you this day. Otherwise, when you eat and are satisfied, when you build fine houses and settle down, and when your herds and flocks grow large and your silver and gold increase and all you have is multiplied, then your heart will become proud and you will forget the Lord your God (8:10–14).

Sacred history tells us that *this is just what happened!*
Again and again generations that experienced God's
blessing became proud, satisfied with their material possessions. And then their hearts strayed from God. The
Book of Judges is actually organized in a series of seven
cycles, each of which begins with a time of blessing.
When blessed with prosperity, God's people lost their
spiritual bearings, turned to sin, and as a result God
permitted them to be oppressed by foreign enemies.
That oppression forced their attention back to God. The
people confessed their sin and prayed, and then God
sent deliverers to free them.

In Psalm 73, Asaph puts the same thing in individual
perspective. Asaph found himself envious when he saw
"the prosperity of the wicked." He says,

> They have no struggles;
>   their bodies are healthy and strong.
> They are free from the burdens common to man;
>   they are not plagued by human ills.
> Therefore pride is their necklace;
>   they clothe themselves with violence (vv. 4–6).

Asaph goes on and on. But finally he sums up his com-
plaint. It's not fair! Asaph has struggled always to please
God, and he has troubles. He's not healthy. He's not rich.
He's forced to carry all the "burdens common to man."
And while Asaph suffers:

> This is what the wicked are like—
>   always carefree, they increase in wealth (v. 12).

But then Asaph had a revelation. He went to the tem-
ple to worship God, and there "I understood their final
destiny."

Asaph realized that what happens in this world is no true measure of divine favor. It is a man's final destiny that counts!

Understanding this, Asaph looked once more at the wealthy wicked he had envied, and realized what God had actually done.

> Surely you place them on slippery ground;
>   you cast them down to ruin.
> How suddenly are they destroyed,
>   completely swept away by terrors!
> As a dream when one awakes,
>   so when you arise, O Lord,
>   you will despise them as fantasies (vv. 18–20).

See it?

The wealthy live on slippery ground. It's so easy, when you have wealth, to forget your need for God. It is so easy to be caught up in a fantasy. A person with enough money to buy anything he or she wants is likely to feel that satisfying his or her desires is what life is all about.

When is material blessing a curse? When wealth draws you into a fantasy world, a world of pleasure and self-indulgence. A world where satisfying your own desires—not serving God and ministering to others—is what life seems to be about.

So it's true.

It isn't fair. It isn't fair that some have such abundant wealth, and others are forced to struggle. But perhaps, just perhaps, the person it's not fair to is the rich man rather than the poor one!

Rich Toward God

What do we find in Jesus' parables about money that helps us think more clearly about wealth and possessions? Here are three of Christ's parables, each with a lesson to teach us:

(1) *Free yourself from the notion that wealth is of ultimate importance.* We all know Jesus' parable about the rich fool (Luke 12:16–21). It's the tale of a rich man whose ground produced an overwhelming crop. He even had to build all new barns to store the overflow. Looking complacently at his stockpile of possessions, the rich man said to himself, "You have plenty of good things laid up for many years. Take life easy: eat, drink, and be merry."

But God said to the man, "You fool! This very night your life will be demanded from you. Then who will get what you have prepared for yourself?"

Suddenly the rich man awoke from the fantasy world created by his wealth to a terrible discovery. Jesus said it plainly. "A man's life does not consist in the abundance of his possessions."

Life isn't a game.

And the person who has the most toys when he dies doesn't win.

He loses!

Why, then, be upset at the unfairness of a life in which you and I aren't rich, while others are?

(2) *Learn the real value of money, and abandon the fantasy.* Many stumble over Jesus' parable of the shrewd manager (Luke 16:1–15). In this story Jesus told of a

manager about to be fired for malfeasance. The manager
called in his employer's creditors and had them falsify
their accounts. Where one owed 800 gallons of olive oil,
the manager had him write 400. Where another owed
1,000 bushels of wheat, the manager had him write 800.
The manager did this so then "when I lose my job here,
people will welcome me into their houses."

Jesus commended the dishonest steward.

No, not for his dishonesty. Jesus commended him because the man understood something that many of us
do not. The steward realized that money is to be used to
prepare for the future. It has no value in and of itself.

And so Jesus told his disciples, "I tell you, use worldly
wealth to gain friends for yourselves, so that when it is
gone, you will be welcomed into eternal dwellings."

The Florida woman who did win that 55-million-
dollar lotto game was a retired schoolteacher well into
her sixties. Wisely, she didn't follow the suggestions of
the "St. Pete Times." Instead, she used her winnings to
set up a charitable foundation. The money she won will
be used to help the homeless, the battered wife, the
abused child.

I suspect she understood what Jesus meant, "You cannot serve both God and Money" (Luke 16:13). The only
thing you can do with money that gives it any value at all
is to use it to serve God.

(3) *Use God's own criteria to measure your relationship with the Lord.* It's a terrible thing to feel that God
doesn't love you just because you're not rich. It's tragic
when we feel we must measure our value to God by the
dollars he has chosen to give us or to withhold. Yet

the story Christ told that shows us God's criteria for measuring personal relationship with the Lord is perhaps the most misunderstood of all his stories. It's the story of workers in a vineyard (Matthew 20:1–16).

You may remember it. A landowner went out early in the morning to hire day laborers. He agreed with them for a denarius, a silver coin that throughout the first century was the standard for a day's pay. Later the landowner went downtown and saw more men standing around because no one had hired them. He set them to work in his vineyard too. About noon he went out again and hired another group. Finally, about five in the afternoon, he hired still more.

When it came time to pay the workers, he gave those who had begun at five a full day's pay—a denarius! Those who had worked all day were delighted. Surely if their employer was giving a full day's pay for one hour of work, they'd get a really big bonus! But when they were paid, all the employer gave them was the denarius they'd agreed on that morning.

Did they howl!

It wasn't fair! "These men who were hired last worked only one hour, and you have made them equal to us who have borne the burden of the work and the heat of the day."

After they quieted down a bit the landowner, who here represents God, simply asked, "Don't I have a right to do what I want with my own money? Or are you envious because I am generous?"

When we think about it, Christ's point is clear. God has not chosen to relate to human beings on the basis of what is "fair." He relates to us on the basis of grace. The true measure of God's love is the free gift he has given us in Jesus Christ. We deserve punishment, but instead God generously forgives us. We earn condemnation, but God grants us eternal life.

You and I are tempted to measure what is "fair" in life by the balance in our bank accounts. But let's remember the stunning reality revealed to us in the gospel. God sent his Son to die that we might have eternal life. And that, my friend, is not fair.

It's not fair at all.

For Meditation and Discussion

1. A recent study of the Florida lottery suggests that people who buy tickets spend much of their time dreaming about what they would do if they won. What might you do if you won millions? Do you think it would help, or harm, your personal relationship with God? Why?

2. Why do you suppose so many people tend to feel the "unfairness" of their personal financial situation so deeply?

3. Read and meditate on Psalm 73 or one of Jesus' parables featuring money. What is the most important message in this passage for you personally?

5

Yours Also
the Earth

Janey Fair was worried. She'd expected fourteen-year-old Shannon home about 11 P.M. She kept peering out the front window of her Radcliff, Kentucky, home.

Janey kept telling herself it was all right. After all, Shannon had just gone on a day trip with the other teens from First Assembly of God. Probably the bus had just broken down. At least, that was what Janey Fair kept telling herself. There was nothing to really worry about. There couldn't be.

Then, at 3 A.M., the phone rang.

Would she and her husband hurry down to the church? There'd been a serious accident. No details. But hurry.

At the church the TV trucks had arrived, and workers were already setting up satellite dishes. In a few hours the entire nation learned of the tragedy that took the life of Shannon Fair and 26 others.

The church bus, bringing 64 teens and three adults home from a day at Cincinnati's King's Island amusement park, was struck by a pick-up truck driven by thirty-five-year-old Larry Mahoney. Mahoney was legally drunk that Saturday night when his truck—going the wrong way on I-71—crashed into the bus. Two hours after the crash his blood alcohol level was 0.24, more than twice the legal level of intoxication. Mahoney had pleaded guilty to drunk driving before, in 1984, and had lost his license for six months.

At the scene officials told parents not to look at the bodies. When the bus was struck, the gas tank had ruptured. "Remember them the way they were," one urged, "the way they are in the pictures in your wallets, and in your hearts."

The next few days are burned into the memories of parents and survivors alike. There were the tears. The funerals. The memorial service at church, where words of hope and faith were uttered. And then all returned to the routine of daily life.

Except that now there was no stirring in Shannon's room when morning came. No rush getting ready for school. No "Hi, Mom," or cheerful sharing of what happened that day when the school bus dropped off other parents' children in the afternoon. There was only a great void, left not only in the Fair home but in so many other Radcliff homes.

And then, Larry Fair and the families learned something else about that tragic accident.

The bus the teens were riding in had been struck in the right front. The force of the blow broke off the bus's suspension, and drove the leaf spring backward into the gas tank, punching a 2½-inch hole. That gas tank was mounted outside the frame, just behind the front door. All the teens who died on the bus were killed by the smoke and fire as gas spewed from that ruptured tank.

Flames flared up through the floorboard, cutting off access to the front door. The smoke was so black and burning that the teens inside couldn't see or breathe. Struggling to reach the only other exit at the back of the bus, stumbling through the narrow aisle, some teens tripped and fell. Others passed out. Within 2 ½ minutes the bus was engulfed by the flames. The 27 teens still inside it were dead.

But why was the gas tank unprotected? Larry Fair discovered that a similar accident had happened in 1972. No one was killed in that accident, but it prompted Congress to pass school bus safety regulations. That legislation was passed in 1974—the year Shannon was born.

But the regulations did not go into effect immediately. In fact, the companies that built the school bus in which so many died—Ford Motor Company and Sheller-Globe Inc.—argued strongly in the '70s against all sorts of safety legislation. Even Lee Iacocca, then with Ford, had complained to President Nixon in 1971, "Safety has nearly killed all of our business."

So implementation of the bus safety legislation passed in 1974 was delayed to April 1, 1977. And the chassis of the bus in which Shannon and her friends were killed was built March 23, 1977, just nine days before the law would have required the gas tank be protected by a metal safety cage.

In fact the chassis of that very bus had holes drilled in the frame—but no cage was bolted on. Larry Fair says bitterly, "Ford would not do anything until the letter of the law absolutely required it."

Within six weeks, Ford representatives came to Radcliff and offered the parents of the dead $700,000 for each victim. Most quickly accepted the money, eager to put the tragedy behind them. But the Fairs, and several other parents, decided to sue. One couple,

Jim and Karolyn Nunnallee, offered to settle for $1—if Ford would recall the thousands of buses built before 1977 that are still on the road, with their gas tanks unprotected, more accidents just waiting to happen. When Ford did not respond to the offer, the Nunnalees also decided to sue. Despite the earlier offer of hundreds of thousands of dollars to parents of the victims, Ford now simply states, "We do not believe our product was defective."

Defective

It's difficult for us to deal with tragedies like those that have affected Sue's life. We sympathize with her pain. But we can see how God has used what happened to Sue for good—for her good, and the good of others.

It's much harder to deal with what happened to Shannon Fair and the 26 others who died in flames while riding a church bus. They were innocent victims. Something clearly is wrong. Something beside the school bus must be defective in any world where such tragedies can happen.

Struggling to believe in a good God despite such occurrences, Christians have offered a variety of excuses. Some have argued that God has nothing to do with such tragedies. He doesn't *cause* them. They just happen. God is as upset about it as the parents, and he suffers with them.

This argument bothers Christians who feel that such a position robs God of his Sovereignty. After all, God *is* in charge. In the verse that gives us the title for this chapter, the psalmist says clearly, "the heavens are yours, and yours also the earth" (Psalm 89:11). That psalm is filled with expressions of God's sovereignty—and of God's faithful love. Somehow, many Christians argue, God must have had a purpose in permitting these young people to die. And so many believers try to offer comfort by saying things like, "God must have loved your child very much, and wanted her to be with him." Sometimes, like Job's comforters, they even wonder aloud, "What could you have done for God to punish you so?"—as though a loving God could even consider punishing mom and dad by creating a holocaust in which a dearly loved child was burned to death.

Others, perhaps closer to the truth, point to realities with which we all have to live. Our world has been cursed by sin. People, not just buses, are defective. The cause of such awful accidents, like the cause of wars, crime, and injustice, is not God, but us!

A friend of Larry Mahoney, named Dwight Hamilton, noted that Larry is a quiet, country-boy type. He likes to hunt coons, drive trucks, and, sometimes, drink. Hamilton told *USA Today* reporters, "He's the type of guy who, when he drank some, he drank quite a bit." But, Hamilton added, "A lot of people do that."

Today Mahoney is charged with 27 counts of murder, facing the possibility of 27 life sentences. Janey Fair says, "He made a conscious decision to get drunk."

And, she adds, "Ford sat in their air-conditioned offices and made a conscious decision to produce unsafe vehicles. They're just as guilty."

Certainly there's something wrong with a world in which a conscious decision can be made to get drunk, and a conscious decision can be made to save a few dollars a vehicle at the risk of human lives. An excuse offered by Tom Butcher, a neighbor of Mahoney's, is no defense. "He's done some things he shouldn't have," Butcher remarked. "But so have I. So let he who is without sin cast the first stone."

But that's just the point!

None of us is "without sin."

We are defective, and yet each of us is fully responsible for the decisions we make and the actions we take. Tragedies like the bus accident near Cincinnati happen because human beings make conscious decisions to get drunk, and officers in corporations make conscious decisions to save a few dollars here and there at the expense of safety.

The fault, as one of Shakespeare's characters says, lies not in our stars but in ourselves.

But we still must face the question of how a sovereign and truly good God could permit such awful things to happen. Even if God does not *cause* human tragedies, couldn't he have prevented them?

Proclaim Freedom

One of the most significant words in the New Testament is a Greek term usually translated "authority" or "power." The word is *exousia*. The underlying meaning of *exousia* is "freedom of choice." The *Expository Dictionary of Bible Words* (Zondervan) explains the relationship of "freedom of choice" to "authority": "The greater the *exousia*, the greater the possibility of restricted freedom of action. A person without *exousia* has little freedom of action, for others maintain a right to control him and determine what he does. A person with maximum *exousia* will have a total freedom of action and thus the right to control the action of others. It is easy to see why, when used of secular authorities, this word commonly means the 'power to give orders' (Matthew 8:9; Luke 7:8; 19:17; 20:20; Acts 9:14; 26:10, 12; 1 Peter 2:13).

"When used of God's overarching authority, *exousia* makes no claims about his inherent strength or nature as God. But it does claim for God ultimate freedom of action. God is totally free to make decisions that cannot be frustrated by any natural or personal power in the universe."

Many passages in the Bible make this claim for God. In Romans 9 Paul argues that God's promises were given freely, not in response to any human act or merit. God chose Jacob to inherit the Covenant promise given Abraham and Isaac, rather than his twin Esau, before the children were born. The choice thus was completely free, unaffected by whatever either twin did later in life.

The amazing thing about God's complete freedom of action, however, is that it *preserves human freedom*. There simply is no analogy from experience for this truth. Whenever human beings gain authority it is at the expense of someone else's freedom of action. A sergeant in the army exercises his authority by giving orders to privates. And in exercising that authority he takes away from the privates some of their freedom of action. If on a hot summer day the sergeant says "march," privates aren't free to go sit in the shade, however much they would like to!

Mom and dad have authority over their children. In exercising that authority, mom or dad takes away some of the freedom that junior had to act. When dad says, "Eight o'clock is bedtime. Off you go," junior can't stay up and watch TV, no matter how much he wants to.

An employer exercises authority over his employees. And, again, in doing so he or she limits the freedom of action of the employee. If the boss says, "Take this tool to the crew out on Lambert Street," the employee can't stay in his air-conditioned office and finish his report, no matter how much he would like to.

In our experience, the exercise of one person's authority, or freedom to act, always has the effect of limiting some other person's freedom in some way.

It's not surprising then, when we think about the Sovereignty of God, or recall that he is the All-Powerful, ultimate Authority in this universe, to be upset when something terrible happens to persons who are obviously victims. We wonder why God doesn't *do* something. If God is Sovereign, if he has authority, he must somehow be responsible for what happened. At the very least he could have done something to prevent it, couldn't he?

The stunning answer to that question is, "No." God *couldn't* have done something to prevent it. And the reason is that God has chosen to exercise his authority in such a way that human freedom of action is always preserved.

We see it in the Garden of Eden. Adam and Eve were placed in an idyllic setting and given complete freedom. They had dominion over all God had created. There was only one restriction. They were not to eat the fruit of a certain tree, a tree called "the knowledge of good and evil."

Even in this Adam and Eve had freedom. They could choose not to eat of the tree. Or they could choose to disobey God and to eat.

They made the wrong choice.

They chose to disobey God, and as a consequence not only did they die, but the defect of sin, which immediately warped and twisted their own nature, was passed down to their children. And to their children's children. And to their children's children's children. Right down to us.

Right down to Larry Mahoney, who drank and then drove his pick-up into a bus filled with young people. Right down to the corporate officers at Ford who decided to risk the lives of the strangers who would ride their buses rather than to spend a few extra dollars and enclose the gas tank with a metal safety cage.

Why did God give human beings such freedom of choice? Because without freedom of choice, you and I and every other person would be something less than human. We would be puppets. Robots. Living out programmed lives without any possibility of making real or significant choices at all. Without freedom of choice we could not have borne that "image and likeness" of God with which the Creator endowed us. God is a moral being who makes moral choices. And for us to be human, to be like God as persons, we too had to have the capacity to choose.

Even if God foresaw that we human beings would misuse our freedom to choose things that are wrong, that are harmful, and that bring pain.

Even if God knew that in the exercise of human freedom one day a pick-up driven by a drunken man would hurtle into a bus filled with innocents, and that 27 of those innocents would die.

God is Sovereign. God is All-powerful. And God has ultimate Authority. But in the exercise of God's authority he has chosen never to infringe on our freedom to choose.

What does all this teach us about the terrible things that happen to innocent people—the terrible things that may well happen to you or to me?

(1) *We are freed from the burden of blaming or excusing God for such happenings.* The burden of blame, where blame is to be fixed, is on those individuals whose responsible choices contributed to the tragedy.

We do live in a defective and sin-cursed world. Because of the flaw in fallen human nature, individuals make thoughtless, wrong, and even vindictive choices that bring pain to others. The deadly downward spiral that began with Adam constantly expresses itself in the lives of individuals and in society as a whole. Rather than cause us to question God, the pain of innocents reminds us how much we need God's help. We need forgiveness for those choices of ours that have hurt others. And we need God's wisdom and enablement, so we can make choices that will benefit rather than cause harm.

(2) *We are reminded of the dreadful burden of freedom.* The foolish person yearns for freedom so he can "do whatever I want!" Yet all that freedom of choice really brings us is responsibility.

We are responsible for the choices we make, not only to God, but to our fellow human beings. We are responsible not to endanger the lives of others by drinking and driving. We are responsible not to make profit our bottom line, but to consider the safety of others. We are responsible. And if, in the exercise of our freedom, others are hurt, it is our fault. Not God's.

Each of us is personally responsible for his or her own choices. No feeble misapplication of that Bible verse, "Let him who is without sin throw the first stone," can hide the terrible fact of our responsibility.

(3) *We are forced to face again the mystery of pain.* No, not just the mystery of our own pain, or the question of why the innocent suffer. We're forced to face the mystery of why God should value our freedom so much that *he* chose to suffer.

The gospel message is that God the Son, the second Person of the Trinity, became a real human being. He lived a human life, died a human death. But his death was unusual indeed. The Bible says that "he was crushed for our iniquities." That "for the transgression of my people he was stricken." That "it was the Lord's will to crush him and cause him to suffer" (Isaiah 53:5, 8, 10). In saying this, Scripture intends us to understand not simply that Jesus paid the penalty for our sins. Scripture intends us to understand also what Isaiah calls the "suffering of his soul" (53:11).

On Calvary the entire weight of human sin crushed the very life from Jesus Christ. It was not just our sinful acts. It was all the pain those acts have caused as well.

Yes, in dying Jesus paid the price for Larry Mahoney's drunken driving. He paid the price for the nameless

Ford executives' calloused choice. But Jesus also knew the panic felt by Shannon Fair in her last moments. He experienced the anguish known by her mom and dad. In that eternal moment hanging on the Cross Jesus suffered *with* us as well as *for* us. There the cries torn from billions of human throats, the tears from billions of human eyes, from Adam until the ages cease to roll, were experienced in their full intensity by Jesus Christ.

And so the mystery remains.

It is not, why would God grant human beings freedom of action, even when he knew the harm that would come to them? The ultimate mystery is why God, absolute in his Authority and with complete freedom of action, would choose to make men free, knowing that the most intense suffering of all would be his own.

For Meditation and Discussion

1. What kinds of events make people ask, "Why would God let this happen?" Make a list, and then ask at least two other persons to answer the same question.

2. The author suggests that to answer such questions we need to understand the unique nature of God's authority and how he exercises it. Can you explain his teaching on authority in your own words?

3. What would it mean if each person accepted full responsibility for the way his choices affected others? Can you think of any way your own life might be different if you always thought carefully about the possible consequences of each choice you make?

6

The Poor among You

God must love poor people," the saying goes, "because he made so many of them."

Whether your voice drips with sarcasm or is lightly tinged with irony, the saying isn't funny. At least, not to the poor.

A year ago the popular cause in the United States was AIDS. Column after column in the newspapers was devoted to this terrible disease, and hardly a network or local newscast failed to mention it. As I write this chapter, the popular cause has become "the homeless." But already the media is tiring of a story they've emphasized—and probably blown out of proportion—for nearly a year. Soon the media focus will shift to something else. But there will still be homeless people in the United States. And there will still be millions of poor. As Jesus said, "You will always have the poor among you" (John 12:8).

Yet poverty, whatever else we may say about it, remains a human tragedy. There's just too much information available on how poverty affects people in our society to see it as anything but a source of terrible injustice.

The poor lack access to adequate medical care and

the balanced diet that promotes health. The poor are those most frequently victimized by crimes of violence. They lack access to those jobs which could lift them out of poverty. Often they are forced together in ghetto-like communities of inadequate housing, amid conditions that breed disease. They are exploited, and often overcharged for the housing they live in and the food they buy at local markets. As a class the poor receive the least effective schooling, and are the least likely to take advantage of any educational opportunities they do have.

I can go into St. Petersburg, Florida, drive through poverty-stricken neighborhoods, and then turn south off Highway 19 to drive past waterfront condos, each of which has slips filled with yachts that cost hundreds of thousands of dollars.

And that just is not fair.

Actually, suggest this to the typical middle class American and the poor receive very little sympathy. The general perception is that most of the poor are lazy. "If they really wanted work, they could find it," is a common argument. Often sympathy for the poor evokes outright hostility. Our taxes are high. How much of the money you and I work so hard to earn is just wasted by government bureaucracies on programs that encourage poor people to sit around and complain instead of making them get off their seats and go to work!

One line of teaching in the Old Testament recognizes the fact that some of the poor *are* lazy! "Lazy hands make a man poor," says Proverbs 10:4, "but diligent hands bring wealth." "Do not love sleep, or you will grow poor; stay awake and you will have food to spare" (Proverbs 20:13). "He who loves pleasure will become poor; whoever loves wine and oil will never be rich" (Proverbs 21:17). "Drunkards and gluttons become poor, and drowsiness clothes them in rags" (Proverbs 23:21). Any person who wastes his time or money is just naturally going to be poor. His condition is a consequence of the poor man's own choices. So it's his problem, not mine.

Not mine. Not yours. And not the government's.

Poverty and Oppression

The problem is, verses that link poverty with personal choices are far less frequent than those that link poverty with oppression.

A number of powerful Hebrew words are used to describe poverty. *Dal*, often translated "poor," is a social term meaning lower social classes that lack the material wealth of the upper classes. *'Ani* pictures a person who is socially powerless and thus unable to resist the powerful in society. The person this word depicts is not only forced to submit to others, he experiences great pain and distress. Frequently English versions translate this Hebrew word as "afflicted." *'Ebyon* portrays a person in desperate need, lacking food and clothing, and without any means for obtaining them. This person is forced to depend completely on others. He is both destitute and dependent. *Rus* also describes deep poverty. It is often used when describing the condition of the lower classes.

Taken together, the Hebrew vocabulary draws a picture of human beings who suffer from far more than the lack of material things. The poor are defenseless, terribly vulnerable to abuses of power. Stripped of many of the rights granted to others in their society, the poor are robbed of the respect due all human beings and robbed of any significant place in their society.

In the Old Testament these words for poor are closely linked with another set of words—words that portray oppression. While some become poor because of laziness or a dissolute lifestyle, most are kept in poverty by injustice. As Proverbs 13:23 observes, "A poor man's field may produce abundant food, but injustice sweeps it away."

Some of the prominent Hebrew terms that describe injustice are *agas, rasas, dak, lahas, 'asaq. Nagas* is a word that describes intense, painful pressure and implies a violent use of authority. *Rasas* is mistreatment, felt as a crushing weight. *Dak* also portrays crushing oppression, while the image contained in *lahas* is that of squeezing the vulnerable. *'Asaq* is misusing power to crush those of lower social status.

What is fascinating, of course, is that all these terms describe the treatment of the poor by society, who because of their poverty are vulnerable. It seems God is not the one who made so many poor people. It seems that man's society is structured in such a way as to both make and keep some people poor. And, again, it's not fair.

Life isn't fair.

Especially to the poor.

No Poor in the Land

Deuteronomy 15:4 makes the striking statement, "there should be no poor among you." Poverty isn't fair, and God is never on the side of injustice. So what God did was to design, within the framework of Old Testament law, a set of social mechanisms intended to root out poverty. Here's a brief description of six ways the Mosaic code deals with the problem of poverty.

Gleaning (Exodus 23:10, 11; Leviticus 19:10; 23:22). When farmers harvested their crops, they were to go through their fields only one time. Anything that was missed, and whatever fell to the ground, was to be left. When the farmer had finished he was to open his fields to the poor, who were then free to gather whatever they could find. Picking the late-ripening fruit, or picking up stalks of wheat that had fallen to the ground, was called "gleaning."

Every seventh year a farmer's land was to be left unplanted. That year the poor were allowed to gather everything the land produced.

Tithes (Deuteronomy 14:28, 29). Every third year a tenth of the crops the land of Israel produced were to be collected and stored locally. This store was to be made available not only to Israel's ministers, but also to "the aliens, the fatherless and the widows."

Capital (Leviticus 25:23, 24). Early Israel's economy was based on agriculture. Originally each family was given its own plot of land. This land was not to be sold, but to be kept in the family. However, if bad times came, the land could be sold *temporarily*. Then, every fiftieth year, the land reverted to the family of the original owners. A person could make a bad business decision or even squander his money, but there was always capital, in the form of land, to give the next generation a fresh start!

Interest-free, forgivable loans (Leviticus 25:35–37; Deuteronomy 23:19, 20). Borrowing money in Bible

times was done in order to obtain necessities, not, as today, to finance purchases. The Old Testament calls on
the wealthy to give interest-free loans to their poor
neighbors. The person who borrowed was supposed to
repay the loan. But if he simply could not get the money
together, God did not permit the debt to weigh him
down forever.

Every seventh year was designated a sabbatical year.
When that year came, outstanding debts were simply to
be canceled! The book of Deuteronomy describes the
impact of the seventh year, and at the same time the
attitude necessary to make God's anti-poverty program
successful.

"If there is a poor man among your brothers in any of
the towns of the land that the Lord your God is giving
you, do not be hardhearted or tightfisted toward your
poor brother. Rather, be openhanded and freely lend
him whatever he needs. Be careful not to harbor this
wicked thought: 'The seventh year, the year for cancel-
ing debts, is near,' so that you do not show ill will toward
your needy brother and give him nothing. . . . There
will always be poor people in the land. Therefore I com-
mand you to be openhanded toward your brothers
and toward the poor and needy in your land" (Deuteronomy 15:7–11).

Equal treatment in the courts (Exodus 23:3, 6; Leviticus 19:15). The Bible recognizes that the poor are powerless, and so specifically protects their legal rights.
Judges are warned not to "pervert justice" by showing
favoritism either to the rich or to the poor. Justice is not
to be influenced either by pity for the poor, or defer-
ence for the rich.

Apprenticeship (Deuteronomy 15:12–18). A poor person who simply could not make it on his own, despite the many provisions made in Old Testament law, had a final option. He might sell his services to another Israelite for a period of seven years. The price he received would enable him to pay off his debts. And, during the seven years he worked for his fellow-countryman, he would in effect learn the skills needed to make his own way.

At the end of the seven years, the apprentice was released from this voluntary form of servitude. The person for whom he worked was told, "do not send him away empty-handed. Supply him liberally from your flock, your threshing floor, and your winepress." In other words, the person who became an apprentice was paid "up front" for his services, was provided for and trained for seven years, and then when he was fully trained was even given capital to enable him to make a fresh start!

So God really meant it when he said, "There *should* be no poor among you." Oh, there were poor. But there should not have been, for God's Old Testament society was designed not only to care for the poor but to do away with poverty!

Blameless and Upright Men

The problem in ancient Israel, as in modern America, is that even the best program of social reform requires a nation populated by upright men. Only generous people, willing to share, can create a just, moral society.

Job was a man like that, who tried honestly to serve

God and who displayed that trait in his relationship with the poor. He says of himself,

> Whoever heard me spoke well of me,
>   and those who saw me commended me,
> Because I rescued the poor who cried for help,
>   and the fatherless who had none to assist him.
> The man who was dying blessed me;
>   I made the widow's heart sing.
> I put on righteousness as my clothing;
>   justice was my robe and my turban.
> I was eyes to the blind
>   and feet to the lame.
> I was a father to the needy;
>   I took up the case of the stranger.
> I broke the fangs of the wicked
>   and snatched the victims from their teeth
>   (29:11–17).

As Job says later, he was a man who wept for those in trouble and whose soul was grieved for the poor (30:25). And Job expressed his concern in practical ways. He reached out with help.

The New Testament picks up the theme of help. In the early church, necessities were distributed to poor believers locally and collections were made when disasters struck distant Roman provinces (cf Acts 6; 1 Timothy 5:1–6; Romans 15:25–28; 1 Corinthians 16:1–4; 2 Corinthians 8:1–7; Galatians 2:10). The writer of 1 John 3:16–18, in a thought echoed in James 2:14–16, confronts Christians with a personal responsibility for those in need. "This is how we know what love is," John wrote: "Jesus Christ laid down his life for us. And we ought to lay down our lives for our brothers. If anyone has material possessions and sees his brother in need but has no pity on him, how can the love of God be in him? Dear children, let us not love with words or tongue but with actions and in truth."

No, it isn't fair that so many are poor.

God's goodness isn't displayed in the pain of those in poverty.

God's goodness is displayed in his design for a society without poverty, and in good men and women like Job, who choose to take the part of the poor.

His Workmanship

Earlier I noted that God uses some unfair experiences to shape character and to equip his people for ministry. While such experiences aren't "good" in the sense of pleasant, they can be "good" in the sense of beneficial. I also suggested that what most people think of as the "good life," of wealth and pleasure, can be spiritually harmful. The fact that some are well off while you and I work for a living may not be fair, but it casts no shadow on God's essential goodness.

It's different with tragedies like the bus fire that took the life of Shannon Fair. Such terrible occurrences aren't "good" by any definition. Yet ultimately God is not responsible for them. The only way that God could create a race in his image was to provide true freedom of choice. The tangled web that humanity creates by misusing freedom is our responsibility, not God's. There is so little comfort to offer when tragedy strikes. All we can do is hurt with those who suffer.

And, perhaps, we can pause to contemplate the wonder that God has chosen, in Christ, to suffer *with* as well as *for* us.

Poverty is something else again.

Poverty is a correctible flaw in the moral fabric of our society.

(1) *Distinguish between correctible and noncorrectible evils.* There's nothing you or I can do about the unfair happenings caused by certain sinful choices. There's nothing we can do to bring back Shannon Fair. But much that is unfair is correctible.

It's not fair that hundreds of thousands of deaths annually are caused by smoking. But our former surgeon general worked actively toward gaining a smoke-free society by the year 2000. One day the members of congress may even muster the moral courage to stop subsidizing tobacco-growers.

It's not fair that no court currently recognizes the rights of the unborn, even though medically there is no question a fetus is *not* "part of the mother's body." The pattern of genes and chromosomes is unique in each human person. And the genetic make-up of the fetus is distinct from that of the mother. One day the courts will recognize the rights of the unborn, even as the courts recognized the human rights of blacks who once were classified as mere property.

Prison conditions here as well as in other parts of the world are deplorable. Groups like Chuck Colson's Prison Fellowship and the Christian Legal Society are working actively not only to minister to convicts, but lobbying to make the entire criminal justice system more fair.

Even poverty, as entrenched as it is in society, remains correctible! The Bible, so clear in its analysis of poverty, contains both social and personal guidelines for helping the poor.

(2) *Act as a responsible Christian citizen.* We do live in a tangled world. Every human society is corrupted by the sinful choices of human beings. But this doesn't mean you and I are to shrug our shoulders, talk about how good things will be after the Second Coming, and ignore correctible evils that make life unfair.

Ephesians 2:8–10 reminds us that while we are saved by grace, once saved we "are God's workmanship, created in Christ Jesus to do good works, which God prepared in advance for us to do." Where life isn't fair to any class of people, God yearns to correct that society's flaw. Even today God displays his goodness through good men and women who are serious about correcting injustices.

(3) *Live as agents of God's love.* I'm not suggesting that every Christian will have the opportunity to do something about poverty. Or about prison reform, or smoking, or abortion on demand. I do suggest that we Christians are called to live in a world where life isn't fair—not as victims, but as agents of God's love.

We're not to lead the chorus of those who complain. We are to be God's agents of change, a people who care, and who, because we care, demonstrate the goodness of our God.

For Meditation and Discussion

1. Imagine that you had the power to develop a whole set of laws designed to rid the United States of poverty by the year 2000. What laws would you hope to pass?

2. Look back at your "not fair" list. How many things on the list are correctible? What would have to happen for them to be corrected?

3. You probably aren't called to lead a crusade to rid society of any particular correctible evil. But wherever we live, there's something every person can do to make a difference. Think about your own community, and your own personal relationships. Then reread Job's words from Job 29. What can *you* do to display the goodness of our God?

7

You Do This to
Your Brothers

Jean put the letter aside, but she couldn't forget the words of her old friend, Dianne.

"Jean, you're one of the most creative and gifted people I know," Dianne had written. "God has given you great opportunities, and I honestly believe you want to please him. That's why I can't understand this thing you're doing now.

"The Bible's so clear on it. First Corinthians 6 says flatly that we are not to take our disputes to court. I honestly don't see how you can get around that passage, or rationalize what you're doing. I urge you, Jean, drop your suit against Karen. Even if she's wronged you as much as you say, and even if she keeps on wronging you, just leave it with the Lord.

"You know, God has ways of dealing with Christians who sin. Remember Ananias and Sapphira? Well, I've known more than a few Christians who refused to repent, and not long after suffered a heart attack! God is the Christian's true judge, you know. Just commit your cause to him.

"Drop the lawsuit, Jean. Please."

Jean and Karen aren't their real names. But the situation is very real, something that is happening to a friend of mine right now. I've changed names, as I've changed other details. But the story I tell in this chapter is true, an extreme example of something not fair in Christian personal relationships.

Most of us will be victims of unfairness in some relationship with a fellow Christian. Usually it will be over something relatively minor: A painter who advertised in the Christian yellow pages, and who not only did a poor job, but after getting his money didn't even come back to finish the trim. A friend who promised to do his share on a project we took on together, but didn't come help— and then insisted that *his* name appear first on the credits. The church we attended and supported so faithfully, that wouldn't let a daughter be married there because we never officially became members.

There are a host of unfair things that happen in the Christian community, as in any association of human beings.

Usually we Christians simply swallow our hurts. After all, it's Christlike to forgive. Besides, we don't like conflict. It's painful to confront someone. It's easier just to let things slide.

The Corinthian church found it easy to let some things slide while being contentious in others. In 1 Corinthians 5 Paul scolds the congregation for permitting a professing Christian, who engaged in sexual immorality, to remain in their fellowship. "And you are proud!" Paul writes in shocked amazement. "Shouldn't you rather have been filled with grief and have put out of your fellowship the man who did this?"

It's clear that in cases where a professing Christian makes sin a practice, it isn't at all Christlike to overlook his fault. Rather, the Christian thing to do is to confront. And the passage makes it clear that among sins calling for confrontation are such things as greed, idolatry, slander, drunkenness, and swindling (1 Corinthians 5:11).

The Christian Thing to Do?

The notion—that it may sometimes be Christian to confront—pains most of us. In general, Christians find it much more comfortable to let things slide.

There are good biblical grounds to justify that attitude. Jesus once used two images to portray the frailty of human nature. He said that people are like sheep, prone to go astray (Matthew 18:10–14). And that human society is like a family, in which the brothers and sisters have constant spats. There's no way we human beings can avoid misunderstandings, hurts, and little family sins (Matthew 18:15). Peter understood what Jesus was saying and raised an important question: How often should he forgive a brother who had sinned against him? Seven times? Jesus told him no, "seventy times seven." Peter understood what that symbolic number meant. The Christian is to keep on forgiving—forever (Matthew 18:21, 22).

Colossians picks up the same theme. We Christians are called to "bear with each other and forgive whatever grievances you may have against one another" (Colossians 3:13). First Peter 4:8 exhorts Christians to love each other dearly, "because love covers over a multitude of sins." Here Peter intends what Paul states so clearly in 1 Corinthians 13. "Love does not take offense." Yes, other Christians will do things to hurt us. But recognizing the frailty of human beings, we can refuse to take offense, keep on loving, and in such a way cover a multitude of sins.

No wonder we shy away from confronting and prefer to remain silent. It's not only easier, it seems to be the pious, the "Christian" thing to do.

On the other hand, we can't avoid that call in Corinthians to confront sin in fellow Christians. And that call reflects a line of teaching woven through both the Old and New Testaments.

The Old Testament concept is expressed in the criminal justice system of Mosaic Law. The Old Testament established no police or criminal court system. Instead, each community was responsible to enforce the biblical code of law. Within the community, elders served as judges of the facts, and each member of the community was responsible to serve as a witness in any case concerning which he had personal knowledge (Leviticus 5:1). More importantly, any citizen who witnessed a crime was responsible to come forward with his information, and to take the role of prosecutor (cf. Leviticus 24:11; Numbers 15:33)!

This responsibility was so significant that Deuteronomy 13:6–11, speaking of idolatry, says, "if your very own brother, your son or daughter, or the wife you love, or your closest friend" should privately urge you to worship false gods, "show him no pity." The evil must be exposed and, in the case of idolatry, the idolator put to death. The passage goes on, "your hand must be the first in putting him to death, and then the hands of all the people."

The community of Israel was to be holy, for God is

holy. And each individual Israelite was responsible to maintain the purity of the believing community.

In Matthew 18, Jesus picks up this Old Testament principle and applies it for his followers.

Jesus taught, "If your brother sins against you, go and show him his fault, just between the two of you. If he listens to you, you have won your brother over. But if he will not listen, take one or two others along, so that every matter may be established by the testimony of two or three witnesses. If he refuses to listen to them, tell it to the church; and if he refuses to listen even to the church, treat him as you would a pagan or a tax collector" (Matthew 18:15–17).

Note that the principle expressed in both testaments remains the same, although the procedures differ slightly. In principle, an individual with direct knowledge of a sin is responsible to act. His goal, as in the Old Testament, is to preserve the purity of the believing community and to maintain harmony between believers. In practice, rather than expose the sin immediately, the person at fault is confronted privately. If the person listens—that is, admits his fault and corrects it—the purity of the community is preserved and forgiveness restores harmony in the relationship. If, however, that person does not listen, the individual with direct knowledge is still responsible to act. He brings two or three others along, and if there is still no response, the matter is brought openly to the church. And then, Jesus said, "if he refuses to listen even to the church, treat him as you would a pagan or tax collector."

Just think. What if, when the temptation of money

and power became too great for Jim Bakker, someone in that organization with first-hand knowledge of the misuse of gifts had said, "Stop"? What if that person had gone to Jim and confronted him? What if he'd even taken the second step, and brought in respected leaders of Jim Bakker's denomination?

Imagine Jim had listened, back then before it was too late.

Ah, what might have been.

PTL might still mean "Praise the Lord," not, as the wags say now, "Pass the Loot." And Jesus Christ might still be glorified rather than ridiculed on TV.

No one did confront.

And no one did speak up.

Or, if they did, they did not follow the whole procedure through. Instead, all too many of those with that first-hand knowledge just . . . let it slide.

Drop It, or Else

Jean and Karen began their business venture as a team. True, Karen was the head of the company, but Jean was deeply committed. They worked together successfully for several years. Their venture kept Karen in the limelight, and soon she was recognized as an outstanding spokesperson in their industry.

Then, based on a series of unfortunate circumstances in Jean's personal life, Karen asked Jean to resign. Jean was deeply hurt when Karen didn't even seem willing to listen to her side. After the break was made, Jean tried to get on with her life. She felt hurt, but no anger. Yet it seemed that every time she tried to make a fresh start, Karen would take some step to block her.

Jean went to a lawyer and explained what had been happening. The lawyer was eager to sue. He identified nearly a dozen violations of the law and of Jean's rights —violations which had not only caused Jean pain but had cost her well over a hundred thousand dollars!

Jean held back. She followed Jesus' prescription to the letter. She contacted Karen and laid out the issues. Karen refused to respond. Jean tried again and again. Finally she suggested binding arbitration, that they let a jury of three Christian lawyers quietly settle the dispute. But Karen refused.

At that time Jean decided simply to let herself be defrauded. It was time to get on with her life. She settled into a new and exciting job, and soon was involved in a work that she was sure would become as exciting and profitable as the first venture.

And then, again, Karen did something that brought pain not only to Jean but also to her family—something that wasn't right, and wasn't fair.

At that point Jean felt she had to turn to the courts. She was now convinced that more than a merely personal issue was involved. Jean felt that what had happened to her involved a serious misuse of power, and that Karen's unwillingness to settle their dispute within the Christian community, as 1 Corinthians requires, indicated a spiritual hardening that could become worse if nothing were done.

And so Jean decided she had to confront—that the only way she could fulfill her responsibility to Christ, to Karen, and to the church, was to take Karen to court.

Today Jean is waiting for a date for the civil case she has brought against Karen to be tried. While she waits, Jean is paying a price.

She has received dozens of letters and phone calls. Some are gentle, many are harsh. Nearly every one tells her to drop the lawsuit.

Nearly all of them, in their letters or phone conversations, have quoted 1 Corinthians 6 and told Jean bluntly that, no matter what Karen may have done, Jean has no right to take a fellow Christian to court.

But are they right? First Corinthians 6 criticizes Christians for taking disputes to non-Christian courts for judgment "instead of" before the saints (6:1). Jean begged Karen to submit to arbitration before an informal court of Christian lawyers. Karen is the one who was unwilling to follow the procedure called for in the New Testament.

First Corinthians 6 asks, "Why not rather be wronged? Why not rather be cheated? Instead, you yourselves cheat and do wrong, and you do this to your brothers" (vv. 7, 8). Jean does feel that she has been wronged. But she also has shown her willingness to be wronged. The continued actions taken by Karen against her, however, have convinced Jean that she has to confront Karen—in court if necessary—for Karen's sake! And for the sake of the church.

As a witness to continuing wrongdoing, Jean is convinced that it is her duty to take a legal action intended not to harm but to cleanse and to purify Christ's church.

As to biblical justification, Jean turns in her Bible to that Matthew 18 passage. If, after following all the procedures Christ has outlined for dealing with a sin in the church, there has been no response, the believer is to treat his erring brother "as a pagan and a tax collector." To Jean that means she is free, as well as responsible, to take Karen, the unresponsive Christian, to court.

Whether or not you support Jean's decision, it's clear that one of the most complex and difficult things for a person to face is a situation in which a Christian says or does something that is not fair. How are you and I to deal with "not fair" experiences within the believing community?

(1) *Be sensitive to human frailties, and willing to overlook hurts.* Most of the "not fair" things that happen to us undoubtedly should be overlooked. Jesus was absolutely right. We are like sheep. And we're like little children within any normal family.

In most cases it's best to follow the Colossians prescription and "forgive whatever grievances you may have against one another" (Colossians 3:13). Most times those "not fair" incidents will involve little things, things that won't harm us or the other person if we simply let love shape our perspective and refuse to take offense.

(2) *Be aware of God's call for holiness, and distinguish faults which call for confrontation.* There are two clues that indicate when to confront. The first clue is subjective. If a brother or sister repeats the "not fair" act again and again, and the repeated acts create a barrier to fellowship, then we need to confront. Christians are called to glorify God in a spirit of unity, "so that with

one heart and mouth you may glorify the God and Father of our Lord Jesus Christ" (Romans 15:5, 6). When that unity is threatened, it's time to confront.

The other clue is objective. If what a person does habitually violates God's standards, then we are obligated to confront. In the United States we tend to think of sex sins as "the" cause for confrontation. Yet the apostle Paul listed along with the immorality that required the Corinthians to confront a sinning brother such ordinary sins as greed, drunkenness, slander, and swindling. One reason for what some have suggested is the spiritual powerlessness of the modern church surely must be our complacent attitude; our willingness to ignore known sins rather than to confront.

(3) *Accept your personal responsibility to take action when confrontation is called for.* There is no question that Scripture fixes responsibility for dealing with the sinful and unfair acts within the believing community on each individual. We may not feel comfortable with that responsibility. But it is ours.

When something happens to you that is not fair, you need to deal with it. Don't let it fester. If it is something that can be overlooked, determine to forget it. Remember that we are all subject to human frailties. Instead of peering constantly at the speck in your brother's eye, deal with those beams in your own.

But if the thing that is not fair reflects a fault that calls for confrontation, then confront. When you do confront, do so in the spirit of Christian love. Remember that you confront not to punish but to cleanse. Not to repay, but to restore.

For Meditation and Discussion

1. List some "not fair" things you have experienced in your relationships with other Christians. From what the author has said in this chapter, what do you think would have been the best way to deal with each situation you listed?

2. Do you think that most Christians follow the course laid out by Christ in Matthew 18? If not, why do you think Christians hesitate?

3. If you were Jean, do you think you would have pursued confrontation to the extent of taking the case to court? Should her motives for taking this course make any difference in the way other Christians evaluate what she has done? Do you think the Christians who have now fired Jean are right or wrong? Why?

4. If any of the "not fair" items on your original list involved actions of other Christians, what do you believe you should do about each now?

8

Woe to Him

Sue was incensed. She'd just returned from a weekend in Orlando, where she'd taken one of those graduate courses teachers are required to take to maintain certification. It had been a fun course, and she enjoyed sharing a room with her friend Lynn. But one thing made her mad.

Before giving the course exam, the professor told the class, "When you take this test, you can use your notes. You can use your textbook. But please don't talk your answers over with anyone. I want this to be your own work." Then he left the room. And three of the teachers seated near Sue immediately got in a huddle and worked through the entire test together!

Sue grew more and more angry. "Just imagine," she thought, "what *they'd* say if their high school students did what they're doing!"

It had happened once before. Sue had dropped out of college when she married. Then after six years Sue enrolled in a small Methodist school about sixty miles from where she and her husband lived. It was hard, being a housewife, commuting, and keeping up with her studies. Near the end of her two years at the college Sue became pregnant. And that didn't make going to school any easier! But Sue worked hard at her studies.

That was why she was so angry when, on final exam day, her professor left the room and the other students in her class grabbed for their books and notes. She stopped working on her exam and looked around carefully. In the class of forty every person beside herself was cheating!

Sue had worked so hard to prepare for that test, even though she was exhausted and the baby kept her awake kicking. So Sue stood up and announced, "If you don't stop cheating, I'm going to tell Dr. Small when he comes back."

She did, too. "I want you to know," she told him, in front of the class, "that when you left, every person in this class cheated on this exam. I studied hard for this final. And it's not fair. If they want good grades, they should study for them just as I did."

And then she watched as the other students scurried up to assure the professor that maybe others had cheated, but "not me!"

Centuries before, Job, too, was upset and angry. His friends, convinced that God was just and fair, held that the disasters which had struck Job were proof he had sinned. They couldn't imagine what Job had done. He always seemed to be a good man. But Job's friends held fast to their theology. If something bad happened to a person, it must be his or her own fault.

Job, knowing that he was not guilty of any grievous sin, struggled with the same problem. How could this be happening to *him*! What had he done to deserve such punishment?

Finally, the unwillingness of Job's friends to accept his claim of innocence drove Job to question the justice of God. Facing facts that religious people often try to dodge, Job reminded his friends of something everyone knows. There are wicked people in this world who prosper. There are evils done that seem to go unpunished. It's fine to believe that God is just and good. But there is precious little evidence of God's justice to be found in this world!

We read a paraphrase of Job's argument earlier:

"Listen. Listen, and then mock. But now listen, and be surprised.

"You talk about the end of the wicked. Well, look around. We each know wicked men who do prosper. They get old. They see their grandchildren. Their houses are safe, nothing bad seems to happen to them.

"God doesn't use his rod on them. Why, they even mock God. They say, 'Why serve God? We're doing all right without him. Where's the profit in prayer?'

"How often do folks like this really get what they deserve?

"Oh, you say, they get it in the end.

"But *when*? Why, God's children seem to suffer more than the ungodly!

"*Who* repays the wicked? Your answers are all lies!"

Job 21:1–34
[author's paraphrase]

Sue shared Job's feelings. The day after Sue confronted her college class, her professor stopped her in the hall. "I want you to know, Sue," he told her, "that I believe you. And you've got your 'A'."

"But that's not the point," Sue said. "It wasn't right. It just isn't fair."

And, because nothing ever happened to those students who did cheat and then lied about it, the sense of outrage—the sense of unfairness—still remains.

Nothing Ever Happened

One of the mistaken impressions that people have about God is that he has good intentions but is powerless to carry them out.

In an earlier chapter I argued that God isn't to blame for the terrible tragedies that strike human beings. Events like the bus tragedy that took the life of Shannon Fair happen because human beings misuse the freedom of choice that God, in order to make a race that is like him in personhood, simply had to provide. God, I suggested, has complete freedom of action. But God does not use his freedom of action to limit our freedom. And even tragedies that cannot be traced directly to sinful human choices are ultimately traceable to Adam and Eve's decision to disobey God.

I suppose that some might take human freedom to imply a powerless God—a God who would like to do good, but can't. Actually, nothing could be further from the truth.

God has *complete* freedom. No matter what choices we human beings make in the exercise of our freedom, God is at work in and through them. And one way in which we see the goodness of God is to understand how he judges persons whose choices are sinful and wrong.

If we truly understood how God even now is judging the unfair and sinful, we could hardly doubt his goodness. In fact, the Bible unveils four principles of present judgment that show us how God is dealing, now, with the unfair. These four principles are moral suasion, human government, dual consequences, and, perhaps surprisingly, kindness.

The principle of moral suasion operates through the conscience of individuals and the community. When Sue spoke up and confronted her classmates, she clearly labeled their cheating for what it was. While they had known that what they were doing was wrong, her stand made it impossible for them to disguise the nature of their actions. They couldn't think to themselves, *Well, I'm really just checking to be sure.* Sue forced them to face the fact that they were "really" cheating.

The Greeks had a fascinating word for what we call the conscience. That word, which is used in the Greek New Testament, is *synedesis.* Originally it meant "looking back." It came to suggest remembering past events and evaluating them by standards of good and evil. In Greek literature and drama the conscience is nearly always portrayed as "bad." The reason is that when we humans do look back and evaluate what we have done, we are plagued by awareness of our failures.

When Sue's fellow students hurried up to the professor to protest their innocence, that act showed they were suffering from an attack of conscience. In exposing their cheating as cheating, Sue stripped away all pretense, and every person in that class stood accused, and condemned, by his or her own conscience.

If you think this isn't judgment, then try recalling a few of the wrong things you've done. Remember them, and sense again the guilt and the shame those memories stimulate.

There is one other aspect to moral suasion, that clear identification of a wrong which takes place when someone stands up for what is right. Such a stand judges not only the individual, but the act. Former Surgeon General Koop had hopes for a smoke-free America, not because he expected laws to be changed, but because the clear identification of smoking as a cause of early and unnecessary death is gradually changing the attitude of Americans. It's no longer "cool" to smoke. Tobacco companies can no longer appeal to teens in ads that suggest smoking is the "grown up" thing to do. Increasingly, Americans realize that smoking is the foolish thing to do, an addiction that can destroy health and rob the smoker of life itself.

It's similar with abortion. Those who have been willing to take a pro-life stand are forcing Americans to face the fact that a fetus is not part of the mother's body, but an independent being, with every potential to become an adult person. In time, moral suasion will change the attitude of the majority, and finally the courts will act to protect the rights of the unborn.

So God is at work now, judging both wicked persons and wicked acts. He is not powerless. And he does not ignore the unfair.

The principle of human government operates through laws and agencies that societies invent for self-protection. Romans 13 puts it this way: Government is "God's servant to do you good. But if you do wrong, be afraid, for he does not bear the sword for nothing He is God's servant, an agent of wrath to bring punishment on the wrongdoer" (v. 4).

Today Larry Mahoney is awaiting trial for killing 27 teenagers. He chose to drink and drive, and the courts will hold him responsible for his actions. Nothing can bring back those teens who lost their lives. But the punishment meted out, if the horror of the tragedy were not message enough, may convey to others the message that Americans simply cannot permit drunks to drive.

Actually, several organizations, from MADD to SADD, are actively working to strengthen laws against drunk driving and to pressure the courts not to treat violations of drunk driving laws lightly.

In the same way, our laws make it possible for the Larry Fairs to press their suit against Ford and hold the company responsible for the product defects that turned what otherwise might have been a minor accident into a holocaust. If major companies will not spend the money needed to make products safe out of concern for the consumer, then such lawsuits may lead them to spend the money to protect themselves from financial liability.

As God's servant, governments, responsible for punishing wrongdoers and enacting laws that protect the public, serve as his agents for good in an unfair and wicked world.

The principle of dual consequences is taught in Habakkuk. Troubled by injustices he saw in Hebrew society about 720 B.C., the prophet had appealed to God. How long would the Lord overlook such wickedness in his people? God answered. He was not overlooking wickedness. In fact, God was raising up the Babylonians, who would sweep down on Judah and carry her people into captivity. God, exercising his hidden but total control of history, would use the free choices made by the leaders of Babylon to punish Judah for its sin.

But then Habakkuk raised another problem. The Babylonians were more wicked than the Jews. How could God let the Babylonians succeed and get away with their wickedness? God's answer, recorded in Habakkuk 2, is succinct. No one "gets away with" wickedness. Even while the wicked seem most prosperous, God is at work to judge them through the psychological and social consequences of their acts.

The psychological consequences of wickedness—the inner aspect of the dual judgment God brings on people who do wrong—are explained in Habakkuk 2:4, 5, in 2:9–11, in 2:12–14, and in 2:18–20. First, the person whose "desires are not upright" may obtain what he thinks he wants, but when he gets it he will be unsatisfied. As a result, he can never be at rest. The more he greedily feeds the flame of his desires, the more dominating his desires become! What a judgment this is. No matter how successful a wicked man appears, inside he is frustrated and dissatisfied (2:4, 5).

Second, the person who "builds his realm by unjust gain" is the victim of fear. As a result he struggles to "set his nest on high, to escape the clutches of ruin." And what a judgment this is! The wicked person, no matter how successful he appears, is anxious and fearful (2:9–11).

Third, the person who "builds a city with bloodshed and establishes a town by crime" is destined to see his hopes come to nothing. Such persons "exhaust themselves for nothing." In the end this earth will be filled with glory of God. All that the wicked work so hard to build will prove nothing but "fuel for the fire" (2:9–11).

Finally, his success leads the wicked man to "trust in his own creation." The rich man trusts in his wealth to protect him; the dictator trusts in guns. But these are mere idols, that in the end will betray the person who trusts in them. In the end, God will judge the wicked. The things in which they trust will betray them.

What a terrible, terrible fate! To possess everything, but to have nothing. To "succeed," but experience no inner peace, no satisfaction. To live a lifetime filled with nothing but unquenched desires and repressed anxiety.

And we sometimes have wondered with Job and Sue why God doesn't punish the wicked!

The other aspect of God's dual present judgment of the wicked is social. This is explained in Habakkuk 2:6–8 and in 2:15–17. The actions of the wicked create hostility in their victims. In time this hostility will be expressed in reprisals. As Habakkuk says, "Will not your debtors suddenly arise? . . . Then you will become their victim" (2:8). The thought is repeated in 2:15–17. The person who seeks to shame his neighbor will himself be overcome by shame. The cup he passes out to others will come around to him, and then his victims will say, "Now it is your turn!"

The principle of kindness is perhaps the most surprising to find in a discussion of divine judgment. But it is important for us to understand. Paul states the principle clearly in Romans 2:2–6. During this present age God is exercising kindness, tolerance, and patience. He is withholding his judgment to give even the most wicked every chance to repent and to find forgiveness.

Yet even God's kindness and tolerance intensify final judgment. Paul says, "because of your stubbornness and your unrepentant heart, you are storing up wrath against yourself for the day of God's wrath, when his righteous judgment will be revealed." Then "God will give to each person according to what he has done."

The image is powerful. Every wicked act is like another stream of water, pouring into a reservoir of wrath, restrained only by the dam of God's kindness. Sometime in the future a day of wrath will come. Then the dam will break, and the wicked will be swept away in a crushing flood of judgment. In that day God's justice will be fully revealed, and no human being will ever again imagine that life is "not fair."

You, Therefore

It's true. Things happen to us in this life that just aren't fair. But God is at work, even though his work may be hidden from us. God is at work to correct the things that aren't taken care of through moral suasion and human government. And God is at work to punish evildoers through consequences that are both psychological and social. Even more, while God in kindness delays the day of final judgment, that judgment day is approaching. And then every inequity will be redressed.

When we are upset, with Job, at the apparent prosperity of the wicked, this gives us something to remember. Life isn't fair. But God is at work judging both wicked acts and wicked people. Looking at reality as God has revealed it, we should perhaps be more moved to sympathy than anger. As God has said, "Woe to them."

One day you and I will see all of life's unfairness openly addressed. What are we to do in the meantime?

(1) *Be willing to take a stand on moral issues.* Some-one has rightly said, all that's needed for evil to triumph is for good men to remain silent. By speaking out on their convictions, and taking a stand, Christians can serve as the conscience of society. Our identification of evil as evil can stir the conscience of others, and our involve-ment can lead to changes in personal and national values.

(2) *Remain confident that God is both sovereign and active despite the unfair things that occur.* God often works quietly behind the scenes. Even though God does not violate human freedom of choice, he works through moral principles deeply imbedded in human nature and reflected in society. Through the moral suasion of good men and women, through wise and just laws, through conscience and human psychology, and through his own patience with those who sin, God is actively correcting the things in life that are unfair. Because we know power in creation and God's love in Jesus, we can trust the Lord to be and to do good, even when life isn't fair to you or me.

For Meditation and Discussion

1. What is difficult about taking a stand against something you feel isn't fair? What are the reasons we should be willing to take stands?

2. The author suggests that God is at work now, dealing with those "not fair" things that have troubled believers from Job to Sue. Which of the principles explaining God's present actions seems most important to you? Why?

3. The author has said very little about final judgment. Read Romans 2:4–6, and then read 2 Thessalonians 1:5–10. According to these passages, what does the fact that God will one day judge human beings have to do with the unfair things in your life?

9

**When the
Dream Dies**

It was 6:30 in the morning, January 24, as I sat down to write this chapter. In just a half an hour Ted Bundy, who murdered at least twenty young women, was scheduled to die in the electric chair.

That morning's *St. Petersburg Times* carried an article on three college students who survived one of his brutal attacks eleven years ago. In part the AP story said:

> Cheryl Thomas was a 21-year-old dance student when Bundy broke into her apartment shortly after his attack at the sorority house a few blocks away. He broke her jaw and severed a nerve leading to her left ear, leaving her with a profound hearing loss and balance problems.
>
> Her injuries destroyed her dream of becoming a professional dancer. She still does not want to talk about the attack, said her mother, Anne Thomas of Richmond, Va.
>
> But Thomas recovered. Although she never returned to Florida State, she eventually earned her bachelor's degree in dance and a master's degree in deaf education. She teaches ballet and works with the deaf. She is married and has a daughter.
>
> "She pulled back. We're really proud," her mother said. "Every day of my life I thank God for her life."

Dreams

Throughout history women have always been most vulnerable to unfairness. Some, like Cheryl, have been able to pull back when their dreams were destroyed. Others, like the young woman in the following story, have not. Her story, one that begins as a romance and ends as a tragedy, teaches us important lessons about how we must respond when life isn't fair.

It begins like a fairy tale; one of those romantic stories that so delights little girls. Our heroine was in love. What's more, she was a princess! And the young man she loved was a poor, but dashing and handsome, young captain in her father's army.

As in all romantic tales the heroine faced difficulties. Imagine how her heart almost stopped when she learned her father wanted her captain to marry her older sister! Imagine her relief when the young captain refused. He was a nobody, he said, unworthy to marry anyone as exalted as the daughter of a king.

Our heroine then began a careful campaign. She told her servants of her love for the young man, sure that word would be carried to her father. Sure enough, the king heard—and smiled in delight. He began his own campaign on her behalf. The king shared with his advisors how much he wanted this young man in the family. He told them that he wasn't interested in the gifts of gold or silver a wealthy suitor might offer. All the king wanted was the young man's strong right arm. Why, the king would consider proof that the captain had killed a hundred of his enemies a more than sufficient gift.

How our heroine's heart soared. Her dreams might yet come true!

As in all fairy tales, this hero accepted the challenge. He took a few of his men and attacked the king's enemies. Bringing back tokens of his victories, he knelt at the king's feet—and declared that he would marry the younger daughter after all.

So they were married. The young captain was promoted to general and went on to win many victories for his father-in-law. And, if this were a fairy tale, we'd end the story here with those familiar words, "they lived happily ever after."

But this is no fairy tale. It's a true story. And the young couple did not live happily ever after at all. The romantic dream of the young princess was, all too soon, destroyed by life's reality.

The princess in our story is Michal [MI-kal]. The king is Saul. And the young army captain is David, destined to become Israel's shepherd king.

Michal's story begins in 1 Samuel 18. The Bible says, "Saul's daughter Michal was in love with David, and when they told Saul about it, he was pleased" (18:20). But Saul was not pleased by any thought of happiness for his daughter. Saul was pleased at the prospect of using Michal's love to murder her lover!

After David killed the giant Goliath he had joined the military. David immediately began to demonstrate his military genius. The Bible says that "whatever Saul sent him to do, David did so successfully that Saul gave him high rank in the army." David also became popular with the people. One song writer even penned a little ditty that had everyone in Israel singing, "Saul has slain his thousands, and David his tens of thousands."

Now, if there's one thing you don't want to do in a monarchy, it's become more popular than the king. Each of David's successes made Saul more angry and jealous of the younger man. Saul, sensing that God was with David, also feared him. And so Saul had a problem. How can a king get rid of a popular young rival without ruining his own reputation?

Michal's love was his answer. He thought, "I will give her to him, so that she may be a snare to him" (1 Samuel 18:21). In challenging David to kill a hundred Philistines, Saul intended that the Philistines kill him!

Saul never gave a thought to his daughter. He didn't wonder how David's death might affect her dreams. Saul, as brutal in his way as Ted Bundy, chose a course of action that was totally unfair to his own flesh and blood.

But David succeeded. The two were married. And David became the king's son-in-law. Michal's dreams seemed about to come true anyway.

Saul's antagonism toward David hardened even more. Finally, the king determined to kill David openly (1 Samuel 19). He sent soldiers to take David in his home, but Michal warned her husband. Loyally she let David down from an upstairs window and he escaped. Then Michal pulled together a pile of clothing and, when the soldiers came, she told them her husband was sick. When the ruse was finally discovered, Michal defended herself as she and David had agreed. She claimed that David had threatened to kill her if she refused to help.

David did escape. For several years he and his men avoided the forces that Saul led out to kill him. Twice

David had a chance to kill the king, but each time he refrained. Yet Saul had his revenge. First Samuel 25:44 tells us that Saul gave "his daughter Michal, David's wife, to Paltiel, the son of Laish, who was from Gallim."

Nearly a dozen years pass before we meet Michal again. Her father, Saul, is dead. David, who has married other women, has been king of the southernmost tribes of Judah and Dan for seven years. All that time there has been war between the south and the north. Finally the commander of the northern army decides to come over to David. His support means that David will at last become king of a united Israel.

David accepts the commander's offer, with one condition: "I demand one thing of you: Do not come into my presence unless you bring Michal daughter of Saul when you come to see me."

It would be nice to imagine that David's demand was motivated by memories of his first love. Perhaps it was. Yet somewhere in David's mind there probably was the thought that his claim to Saul's throne would be strengthened as the old king's son-in-law. Whatever David's motives, his demand was met. In the north they "gave orders and had her taken away from her husband Paltiel son of Laish" (2 Samuel 3:15).

Whatever David's motives, no one asked Michal what she wanted. No one went to her and said, "You've been married for a dozen years to Paltiel. Do you want to go back to David after all this time?" In failing to consider Michal's feelings, David was treating her as cruelly as Saul had treated him. Michal was a victim, and it just was not fair.

We don't know the nature of the relationship between Michal and Paltiel. Yet one sentence in the biblical text is suggestive. Second Samuel 3:16 says that "her husband went with her, weeping behind her all the way to Bahurim." Until finally he was told, "Go back home." And he went.

The last chapter in Michal's story is found in 2 Samuel 6. David has been crowned king and has made Jerusalem the capital of a united Israel. Intent on making Jerusalem the religious center of his realm as well, David has decided to bring the ark of the covenant there. This, the holiest object in Israel's faith, symbolized the living presence of God with his covenant people.

When the great day came, David was excited and thrilled. That day he laid aside his royal robes. Dressed only in a simple linen ephod, like that worn by the priests, David led the procession that accompanied the ark. He was dancing and leaping and praising God.

By an upstairs window in the royal palace, Michal stood watching. The Bible says that "when she saw King David leaping and dancing before the Lord, she despised him in her heart" (2 Samuel 6:16). The romantic dream of her youth was completely dead, replaced by contempt and scorn. When David returned to the palace Michal confronted him. Her voice dripping with sarcasm, Michal said, "How the king of Israel has distinguished himself today, disrobing in the sight of the slave girls of his servants as any vulgar fellow would" (v. 20).

Coolly David replied, "It was before the Lord, who chose me rather than your father or anyone from his house when he appointed me ruler over the Lord's people Israel—I will celebrate before the Lord. I will become even more undignified than this, and I will be humiliated in my own eyes. But by these slave girls you spoke of, I will be held in honor" (vv. 21–22).

The next verse is the last mention of Michal in the Old Testament, and serves as her epitaph. "And Michal daughter of Saul had no children to the day of her death" (v. 23).

Destroyed Dreams

To me Michal is one of the most tragic of all the people of the Bible. She began life as a princess, dreaming romantic dreams, dreams that never came true. The two men she trusted most, betrayed her. Her father knew of her young love, but cruelly chose to use her as an instrument of revenge. Her first husband, David, wanted her back—but showed no more concern for her feelings than her father did. He used her too.

It's no wonder that Michal's heart was filled with bitterness as she watched David celebrate his relationship with God. It's no wonder that the love she had once felt turned to contempt. Life hadn't been fair to Michal. Her father hadn't been fair. David hadn't been fair. All her dreams had been destroyed. And so Michal closed her heart, unwilling to risk being hurt again. She lived the rest of her life alone, with no husband's arms around her. No child reached out to her, eager to snuggle on her lap.

Michal illustrates one way that you and I can respond to life's unfairness. We can become bitter. We can despise the people who hurt us. We can withdraw. Or, like Cheryl Thomas, we can pull back.

We can build a new life on the ashes of our dreams. We may never dance as we once imagined, and hear the cheers of the multitudes. But perhaps like Cheryl we can teach others to dance. We can learn to celebrate life as it is, even when life is not as we dreamed it would be.

What lessons for living do we learn from Michal, the princess whose fairy tale ended in tragedy? Three things:

(1) *We learn to keep looking for God.* The saddest thing in Michal's story is that as the citizens of Jerusalem celebrated, Michal never saw God's ark.

You and I must learn to look beyond the people and events that hurt us, and remember who God is. This is the significance of the ark before which David danced. It was the symbol of God's presence. It was the symbol of his deliverance of Israel from slavery in Egypt. In it was a peck of the manna God supplied his people in the wilderness, reminding Israel that he was committed to meet their needs. In it, too, were the stone tablets on which God had written the Ten Commandments, his revelation of the lives God expected his people to live. The lid of the ark served as the mercy seat, the place where once a year the high priest spilled the sacrificial blood which reminded all Israel that God forgave their sins.

All that God was to Israel was symbolized in the gold-covered chest before which David danced.

And Michal, bitter and angry, never caught in that symbol of Israel's faith even the slightest glimpse of God.

Hebrews 12 reminds us that when hardships come, we are to view them as a loving gift from God. Reality strips our dreams away, but in all that happens "God is treating you as sons." Hardships are intended as discipline, meted out "for our good, that we may share in his holiness. No discipline seems pleasant at the time, but painful. Later on, however, it produces a harvest of righteousness and peace for those who have been trained by it" (12:7–11).

The Hebrews passage goes on to teach us how to reap these benefits. "Make every effort to live in peace with all men and be holy," the writer says. And, "see to it that no one misses the grace of God and that no bitter root grows up to cause trouble and defile" (12:14, 15).

In her pain, Michal missed the grace of God. The ark passed before her, but failed to remind her that God was a God of love. So Michal surrendered to bitterness. And, as a result, she lived the rest of her life alone.

(2) *We learn to remain vulnerable.* Michal's early romantic dreams had been shattered, just as Cheryl's dreams of a career in dance were dashed by Ted Bundy's vicious attack. Yet somehow Cheryl remained vulnerable to life. She returned to college. She even turned her deafness to advantage, obtaining a master's degree in deaf education. She married. She had a child. And despite problems with her balance, today she even teaches ballet.

Life is hard on all our dreams. But we must remain vulnerable. We must be willing to keep trying, and in trying, open ourselves up to fresh hurts. In Cheryl's mom's words, we must "pull back."

Michal, unable to sense God's grace in her tragedies, was unable to deal with life any more. How do we know? We see it in the cause of her contempt for David. His celebration of God was "undignified," in her opinion. In setting aside his royal robes, she felt David failed to act as a king should. Her dreams shattered, all Michal cared about now was appearances. The contempt she felt for David now was caused by his failure to fulfill the role she thought appropriate to a king.

You and I have to avoid any retreat to appearances. We must face life as it is, caring about people, willing to risk, even though in so doing we become vulnerable to further hurts.

(3) *We learn to forgive, and to accept forgiveness.* Michal was hurt by the two men she had the greatest reason to trust. One of the things that you and I learn as our dreams are destroyed is that even those we love the most are fallible. All too often they will cause our deepest hurts and provide the most telling reminders that life is not fair.

When that happens, we must remember how frail every human being is. None of us has escaped the damaging power of sin. None of us is ever totally pure, ever completely loving. And because all human beings have been warped by sin, each of us will hurt others and be hurt in turn. And this is especially true of those we love.

I have no excuse to offer for David's treatment of Michal. It wasn't fair. Yet David was a man who truly loved God and honestly tried to please him. If Michal had only come to David and shared her pain—if she had been willing, as another woman David mistreated was willing to forgive—Michal's life might have been redeemed. But rather than make allowances, rather than forgive, Michal became bitter. And in her bitterness Michal condemned not David, but herself.

How much you and I need the healing that comes with forgiveness. We need the release that comes when we forgive a person whose treatment of us has been unfair. And we need the peace that God provides when we accept forgiveness from those whom our acts have harmed.

For Meditation and Discussion

1. Are you more like Michal or Cheryl Thomas? In what ways do you resemble the person you chose?

2. Carefully read Hebrews 12:5–15. Underline verses or phrases that you think would be helpful to anyone in Michal's place. Then go back over each underlined phrase. How might Michal have applied each truth, and what difference would it have made?

3. What dreams of your own have been destroyed? How did it happen? If your response has been one of bitterness, read Hebrews 12 over again for yourself. What verses apply especially to you? How will you apply them, and what difference will they make now?

4. For a study of another woman hurt by David, and what happened to make her story one of triumph rather than tragedy, see chapter 4 of *When People You Trust Let You Down: Experiencing God's Faithfulness* (Word, 1987).

10

**The Thing That
I Feared**

In Leo Rosten's *The Joys of Yiddish,* the author re-counts a story about a legendary *zayde* (grandfather) in "Shpolle," who was called "the Saint of Shpolle." Rosten says, "He was said to have become so heartsick over the sufferings of the Jews and the injustices of the world that he decided to put God on trial. So he appointed nine friends as judges, himself being the tenth needed for a *minyan,* and summoned the Almighty to appear on the witness stand. (Since God is everywhere, the *zayde* simply closed his door.)

"For three days and nights this remarkable juridical body tried the Lord: They presented charges, devised defenses, pondered, prayed, fasted, consulted the *Torah* and the *Talmud.* Finally, in solemn consensus, they issued their verdict: God was guilty. In fact, they found him guilty on two counts: (1) He had created the spirit of Evil, which He then let loose among innocent and pliable people; (2) He clearly failed to provide poor widows and orphans with decent food and shelter."

To many, the story might have a sacrilegious ring. But the fact is, most human beings have also tried God, in the court of their own heart. And, like the ten Jews in Rosten's story, most have also found him guilty.

Despite our first impressions, the biblical story of Job powerfully reflects this theme.

Job, Retold

You remember the dramatic story of Job. In Act One (Job 1:1–2:10), Job is introduced as a "blameless and righteous man." In the very first scene, Satan, "the spirit of evil," reluctantly comes with all other angelic beings to report to the Lord. God specifically points out Job. "Have you considered my servant Job?" the Lord asks. "There is no one on earth like him; he is blameless and upright, a man who fears God and shuns evil."

Satan immediately challenges God. Job is well rewarded for his piety. God has put a hedge around this servant of his, so no harm can touch him. If God would only remove that hedge, Satan could make Job curse God aloud!

God responds by removing the hedge. Satan can do what he wishes to Job, but he cannot touch the man himself. The tragedies that Satan causes strip Job of his wealth and of his ten children in a single day. The timing and nature of the tragedies convinces every witness that God himself must have brought the calamities upon Job. But Job, despite his doubts, actually falls to the ground and worships! "In all this," the Bible says, "Job did not sin by charging God with wrongdoing" (1:22).

In the next scene the angelic hosts again appear before the Lord, and God again asks Satan, "Have you considered my servant Job?" Again Satan challenges the Lord: "A man will give all he has for his own life. But stretch out your hand and strike his flesh and bones, and surely he will curse you to your face" (2:5). Again God gives Satan permission to act against Job, and this spirit of evil "afflicted Job with painful sores from the soles of his feet to the top of head" (2:7). Even Job's wife now urges him to curse God and die. Job refuses, and this act of the drama closes with the statement, "in all this, Job did not sin in what he said" (2:10).

But inside, Job's swirling thoughts were filled with doubt and despair.

Act Two of the drama (Job 2:11–31:40) begins when three friends arrive to comfort Job. They are so shocked at his suffering that for a whole week they simply sit with him in silence.

But then they begin to probe. Hesitantly at first, and then more and more forcefully, they offer their advice. Everything the three friends say is based on certain assumptions about God. First, the terrible things that happened to Job have been caused by God. Second, God is just and fair; therefore what has happened cannot be unfair. Third, God is a moral judge, and judges sin. Thus, Job's suffering is punishment for sin. Fourth, a sinner can repent, turn to God, and find forgiveness. Fifth, when a person has reestablished his relationship with God the punishment will be lifted. Sixth, when a person maintains a right relationship with the Lord, no evil can befall him.

Based on these assumptions about God, Job's friends conclude that Job has committed some terrible sin and deserves punishment. With great determination they attack Job's integrity, intent on forcing Job to confess his sin so he can be restored.

Job himself is in turmoil. Job knows that he has committed no grievous sins. He has been sensitive to God; he has constantly tried to please him. Yet Job's theology is the same as that of his friends! Job has no way to explain what has happened to him. And so, in all honesty, Job reaches the conclusion that God is not fair after all! Like the ten Jewish elders of Shpolle, Job believes that God is guilty. And it is this, rather than his suffering, that causes Job to despair.

If a human being can't trust God, there is no hope at all. If a human being can't trust God, the only realistic way to view the future is with trembling and fear.

Act Three (Job 32:1–37:24) opens after Job and his three friends have argued for days. Job has stubbornly defended his integrity. Despite his anguish, portrayed so powerfully in 30:20–31, Job maintains that he is a good man, even if his claim implies unfairness on the part of God.

It is at this point, when Job and his friends finally fall silent, that a younger man named Elihu speaks up. Elihu agrees that it is "unthinkable that God would do wrong, that the Almighty would pervert justice." But he still says to Job, "I want you to be cleared."

He does clear Job, by the simple act of suggesting that God may have had a good reason for permitting Job to suffer. God sometimes brings suffering, Elihu says, "to turn back his soul from the pit, that the light of life may shine on him" (33:29,30). That is, God may use suffering to *instruct* human beings as well as to *punish* them!

When a good man suffers it is not necessary to assume that he is being punished for sin.

In suggesting this one alternative reason for suffering, Elihu opens up the possibility that God may have many different reasons to permit the injustices that so often make life unfair. Elihu does not try to explain the reasons. But by breaking through assumptions that limited Job's own understanding as well as that of his three friends, Elihu made it possible for Job's friends to accept his claims of innocence. And Elihu has made it possible for Job to trust.

God himself appears in Act Four (Job 38:1–42:6). God does not explain his motives. Instead he speaks of his own greatness in contrast to human frailties. Now fully aware it is not the place of the creature to question the wisdom of the Creator, Job bows before the Lord:

> My ears had heard of you
>   but now my eyes have seen you.
> Therefore I despise myself
>   and repent in dust and ashes.

Finally, the play is over.

But the author has one final word. Stepping out from behind the curtains, he tells the audience what happened then to Job and his friends (42:7–17). God was angry with Job's friends, because they "have not spoken of me what is right, as my servant Job has." Only Job had been willing to face the fact of his innocence, and to struggle with doubts about God's fairness. The kind of piety which ignores reality is never honoring to God.

Job is permitted to pray for his friends, and they are forgiven. As for Job, his fortunes are restored. His wealth is doubled, and he has seven more sons and three more daughters.

There is a subtle but beautiful suggestion here. Job's wealth is doubled. But he is given only ten more children. Why? Because in fact his family was doubled too. The ten who died were not lost. It was only their life on earth that had ended. They were with the Lord, and Job would see his children again.

God on Trial?

Earlier I said that underneath the surface, God himself is on trial in the book of Job. I also said that God has been tried in most human hearts—and found guilty.

What do I mean?

First of all, no one can live very long before he or she becomes aware that life isn't always fair. That realization has to affect us. We may loudly affirm our conviction that God is just and good. But we are constantly confronted with evidence that calls this conviction into question.

Like the elders of Shpolle we see the spirit of evil at work in the land, and we know that poor widows and orphans are not provided with decent food and shelter. Job's friends argued desperately against Job's claims of innocence because they (wrongly) believed that God's goodness could only be vindicated by proving, somehow, that what happens to human beings in this life really is fair. On the other hand, Job honored God by facing reality and admitting that life isn't fair, even though his admission caused him to question the justice of the Lord.

In the story of Job, it is not Job who is on trial. It is God.

Second, there is evidence in the book that God had been tried in Job's secret heart—and found guilty—long before his troubles began!

In Job's very first speech he expresses his despair and then utters this revealing cry:

> What I feared has come upon me;
>   what I dreaded has happened to me.
> I have no peace, no quietness;
>   I have no rest, but only turmoil.
>   Job 3:25,26

Do you see it? "What I feared has come upon me." Job, whose life was blameless and upright, who tried always to please God, was fearful of the future. He was afraid that the God he worshiped would let something terrible happen to him, *even though he had been good!*

In his heart of hearts Job had tried God and found him guilty. It was because he felt he could not trust God to do good that Job had dreaded the future. Even though Job himself was upright. Even though Job himself had been so blessed.

In this book I've tried to deal with some of the issues that led the elders of Shpolle to try and to convict the Lord. The "spirit of evil" is found not only in Satan, but in human beings. We are not really "innocent and pliable people." God has given man freedom of choice, and we human beings have used our freedom to cause pain and to institutionalize injustice. God is not responsible for the actions of Satan or human beings, even though God uses sinful choices to accomplish his own ultimately good purposes.

Yet all the philosophical and theological answers we

might marshal are inadequate to deal with the doubts and fears that take root in our hearts. Job worshiped God. Job believed, consciously, that God was fair and good. And yet in his heart, Job had actually convicted God of unfairness. It was this verdict by Job's inner court that had made him fear the future despite the many blessings that were his.

You and I may also believe, consciously, that God is fair and good. Yet in our hearts we too may have already convicted God—and express that inner verdict as fear of the future.

How are you and I to deal with this, the inner courtroom? What can you do to free yourself of fear, and develop a truer trust in the Lord?

(1) *Open yourself to pain.* Yesterday I took little Sarah, our eight-year-old, to have a blood test. She looked at the needle used to draw blood, and stiffened in fear. The nurses tried to reassure her. It would only be a pin prick. It would hurt only for a moment, and then hardly at all. But Sarah at eight refused to hear and struggled against the coming prick.

How like Sarah we are as we look ahead and imagine how terrible our pain might be. We fear sickness. We fear the loss of jobs. We fear for the future of our children. We fear what others might think or do.

Being a Christian provides no protection against pain. What it does provide is expressed in this assurance found in Romans 8:28. "We know that in all things God works for the good of those who love him."

This does not mean that pain is ever good in itself. The unfair in life is always wrong. Yet, somehow, God is great and wise and powerful enough to bring good to those who love him from life's "all things."

We told Sarah not to be afraid, that it would only hurt a little bit. We told her that through the blood test good would come.

I can't tell you that what lies in your future will only hurt a little bit. But I can tell you that, because God is both Almighty and truly Good, he will see to it that through your suffering good will come. Whatever the future holds, God will be there for you. He will stay with you. And God will use the unfair things in your life for good.

(2) *Look for the good in your relationship with God.* God never explained to Job what good he intended to bring through Job's suffering. It is significant that Satan suffered his defeat in chapter 2, yet Job's suffering continued for weeks. Somehow God was committed to transforming the evil that Satan had done into good.

Perhaps we catch a glimpse of God's purpose in the fact that, through the dispute with his friends, Job finally faced and expressed his doubts and fears. Only then did God reveal himself more fully to his servant. Then, overwhelmed by his awareness of God's greatness and glory, Job said, "My ears had heard of you—but now my eyes have seen you" (42:5).

Suffering frequently has this effect on believers. We have heard of God. We believe in him. But when pain comes we experience the Lord in fresh, new ways. Often it is only after some great tragedy that we can say, with Job, "now my eyes have seen you."

If you and I look for the good that God promises in externals, we're sure to be disappointed. I can't argue that Ted Bundy's vicious attack on Cheryl Thomas, an attack that destroyed her dream of dancing professionally, was "good." I can't argue that the life she now leads is better than the one she would have known. I can't argue that, because I just don't know.

I do know, however, that if you and I open our lives to suffering, and open our hearts to God, God will draw near. We will *see* where before we have only *heard*. And everything that deepens our personal relationship with God is good.

(3) *Meditate on the suffering of Christ.* There are so many benefits for us here. In Christ we see that suffering really can be an expression of total commitment, of matchless love. In Christ's suffering we are reminded again and again that God's only desire is for our good.

Perhaps Romans 8 says it best. Paul has expressed his conviction that God works in all things for the good of those who love him. He goes on:

"What, then, shall we say in response to this? If God is for us, who can be against us? He who did not spare his own Son, but gave him up for us all—how will he not also, along with him, graciously give us all things? . . . . Who shall separate us from the love of Christ? Shall trouble or hardship or persecution or famine or nakedness or danger or sword? . . . . No, in all these things we are more than conquerors through him who loved us. For I am convinced that neither death nor life, neither angels nor demons, neither the present nor the future, nor any powers, neither height nor depth, nor anything else in all creation, will be able to separate us from the love of God that is in Christ Jesus our Lord" (Romans 8:31–39).

As we contemplate this love, splashing out on us through the Crucified One, God will quiet our fear of the future. In our inner heart the court will again convene, and this time, the verdict will be "Innocent."

God is not unfair!

Then, with our trust completely in God, we will face the future pain with confidence and at peace.

For Meditation and Discussion

1. Do you think of yourself as an anxious or fearful person? What indicators can you think of that suggest either you are an anxious person, or that you are not?

2. Do you think most Christians would be more comfortable arguing Job's case, or the case of Job's three friends? Why?

3. The author suggests that fear of the future indicates a person has tried God in his heart, and found God guilty of unfairness. He also suggests three things we can do to change that inner verdict. Which of the three suggestions do you think is most helpful? Which would be hardest for you to follow? Why?

11

All Spiritual
Blessings

I can't resist sharing another of Leo Rosten's stories from *The Joys of Yiddish*. He says it is one of the oldest of Jewish stories. It concerns a poor man "who came to his rabbi and complained that he was living in one room with his wife and four children and *machetayneste* [mother-in-law]—and the congestion was impossible to bear any longer."

"Do you have a goat?" asked the rabbi.

"Yes."

"Take it into the room."

"*What!*"

"Do as I say."

So the poor man went home and brought the goat into his house.

A week later he hurried to the rabbi, sputtering: "I did what you asked. I took the goat in, and things are even worse than before! Rabbi, what shall I *do?*"

"Do you have any chickens?" asked the rabbi.

"Yes. Three—"

"Bring them into your house."

"Rabbi!"

"Do as I say."

So the poor man brought the three chickens into the

house, and a week later returned to the rabbi, wringing
his hands.

"It's terrible! I can't stand it any more!"

"Put out the goat," said the rabbi.

The poor man did as he was told and came back. "It's a
little better, rabbi, but three chickens in a room with
seven people . . . ."

"Throw out the chickens," said the rabbi.

And finally the man stood before the rabbi, over-
joyed: "Rabbi, there's no one as wise as you! My house is
now a paradise!"

I suspect that God has been using the wise rabbi's
technique since the beginning of time. God understands,
as we so seldom do, that contentment is a matter of
perspective. So many of the unfair things that happen to
us serve as the shadows which, as in a master painter's
work, direct attention to features bright with light. You
and I can focus our attention on the unfairness that
crowds in around us, until like the poor man, we feel life
is unbearable. Or we can let the pain of the unfair serve
as a contrast that helps us appreciate the good things in
our lives.

Perhaps this is implied in Paul's prescription for contentment, found in Philippians 4. "Don't be anxious
about anything," he writes, "but in everything, by prayer
and petition, with thanksgiving, present your requests to
God. And the peace of God, which transcends all understanding, will guard your hearts and your minds in Christ
Jesus" (vv. 6, 7).

Notice that Paul doesn't tell us to express thanksgiving
for everything. He says *in* everything.

Whatever happens to us, life still has its highlights.

We can petition God in our problems. But we only gain perspective by remembering, at the same time, those many things for which we can be thankful.

Thankfulness, which puts life's unfairness in perspective, brings us an inner peace that "transcends all understanding," and guards our hearts and minds in Christ Jesus.

Jacqui-Kess Gardner, of Baltimore, Maryland, shared this experience with Abigail Van Buren. I read her letter in the *St. Petersburg Times.*

Dear Abby. We hear so little that is hopeful and good these days, I want to share a story with you.

Five and a half years ago, our son, Jermaine, was born blind, with no nose and severe deformity of the forehead. The doctors told us that he was also deaf and probably would be retarded.

Doubting my ability to raise such a child, I planned to leave him at the hospital and give him up to be raised in an institution. But my mother persuaded me to take him home instead.

As it turned out, the doctors were wrong. Although Jermaine was blind, he was highly intelligent, and instead of being deaf, he possessed a level of hearing that was especially acute.

We first suspected that Jermaine was an "unusual" child when he was only 5 months old. When his brother, Jamaal, who was 5 years older, practiced the piano, Jermaine would keep perfect time with his foot. He loved music and would crawl to the piano every chance he got.

We started giving him piano lessons when he was 2½ years old, and he was soon playing everything his brother played. Weekday mornings Jermaine now goes to a neighborhood school to learn Braille. The rest of his day is spent at the piano.

Jermaine's teacher, Jack Beyers, who was also a child prodigy, has plans for him—geared toward a concert career. Jermaine has already played with Stevie Wonder, and he's scheduled for concerts in Miami, London, and Japan in 1989. He's also doing a Donahue show.

The National Craniofacial Foundation offered to finance the $250,000 required to remodel Jermaine's face in a series of operations. American Airlines is donating the plane tickets, and the Sheraton Hotel will put us up free while we are seeing the doctors in Dallas.

The Piano Technicians Guild of Baltimore has given Jermaine a beautiful baby grand piano.

Abby, please let your readers know about the National Craniofacial Foundation in Dallas. It acts as a clearing house, referring patients to more than 20 qualified centers across the country. It provides financial assistance and helps families cope with the psychological stresses they are bound to feel when they have a child born with severe facial deformities.

People all over the world have been incredibly kind, and we are eternally grateful.

How often we try to avoid the unfair in life. Like Mrs. Gardner we're tempted to leave our trials, as an unwanted child, for someone else to bear. But if we do, we miss the unexpected joys that accompany life's difficulties. All too often we miss experiences that have the potential to make us, too, eternally grateful.

I don't want to sugar coat life's unfairness. Not every experience will be brightened by such highlights.

Last Friday my sister called. She told me that my cousin, Tom, with whom I'd grown up, had died. Tom was a blond, lanky boy. We often played together as children. Tom grew up to be a tall, handsome man. He had a gift for selling. In his late twenties he opened a successful dealership to sell the heavy equipment used by construction firms. He married Elaine, a small, attractive brunette.

Then Tom was diagnosed as having a disease closely related to muscular dystrophy. Within a few years he was unable to work, unable to walk. His condition deteriorated rapidly. Elaine took their savings and bought a small neighborhood store in a Chicago suburb. She and Tom lived upstairs and, because there often wasn't enough money to hire a clerk, Elaine operated the store and took care of my cousin.

I cannot even imagine the strain that Elaine has lived under these past twenty years. For many of those years Tom has been unable to feed himself; these last years Tom has hardly recognized his wife, and has not known his mother or dad. And yet Elaine has remained faithful. She has fed and washed and cared for the man she took "for better or for worse" so many years ago.

For people like Elaine, the dark strokes on the canvas dominate. As in a Rembrandt portrait, even the highlights are cast in shadow.

It's not easy in situations like hers to find reasons to be eternally grateful.

Eternally Grateful

John Donne, ill with what he thought was the Black Death that decimated Europe in 1623, wrote a series of meditations. One contains this prayer: "O eternal and most gracious God, you have reserved your perfect joy and perfect glory for the future, when we will for the first time know you as we are known. In an instant we will possess, forever, all that can in any way conduce to our happiness. Yet here also, in this world, you grant us earnests of that full payment, glimpses of that stored treasure. Just as we see you through a glass darkly, so also do we receive your goodness by reflection and by your instruments."

Here Donne touches on two realities that bring us Christians a unique perspective on the unfair in our lives. Anyone can see the wisdom of focusing on the positive in life, of being thankful for highlights. Anyone can feel uplifted when he or she reads of the good things that have happened to Jermaine. But only a Christian can look at situations like Elaine's and see the goodness of God.

The two realities that can give a Christian unique perspective are: the priority of spiritual blessings, and the certainty of future joy.

Spiritual blessings. The apostle Paul launches the book of Ephesians with praise to God, "who has blessed us in the heavenly realms with every spiritual blessing in Christ" (1:3). The chapter goes on to identify some of these blessings.

• God chose us in Christ before the creation of the world to be holy and blameless (1:4). Holiness and blamelessness are not highly prized by the people of this world. But they are important to God. Even the most painful of our experiences contains blessing if, in submitting to it, we let God shape our character to be more like his.

• God has predestined us to be adopted as his sons through Jesus Christ (1:5). Whatever happens to us here, we know that we are God's own children now. Nothing can destroy that relationship; nothing can weaken his Father love.

• In Christ we have redemption; the forgiveness of sins (1:7). God has dealt with our sins. We are freed from the burden of our past failures. We are released from the guilt that kept us from feeling good about ourselves, and kept us from experiencing intimacy in our relationship with the Lord.

• God has revealed the future to us (1:9, 10). We know that this life is not the end. We live in hope, not in the desperate search for "gusto" driven by fear that "we only go around once in life."

• God has selected us to be his chosen people (1:11). God knows you and me as individuals, and he has proven his love for us by selecting us to be his own.

• God permits us to glorify him (1:12). The way we bear our trials brings glory to God. The way we respond to life's unfairnesses—our loyalty, our faithfulness, our courage, gentleness, and kindness—demonstrates to the universe the grace of a God who is able to make lost human beings truly good.

• God has marked us with his seal of ownership (1:13, 14). We know, no matter how dark our days, that we belong to God. He is with us through his Holy Spirit. We are his prized possessions. And God will keep us safe until the day of redemption finally comes.

These and the many other spiritual blessings we have in Christ may mean little to the unbeliever. But they are life's anchor to the Christian. Possession of these spiritual blessings brings us an inexpressible and glorious joy that exists independent of our circumstances. If you have ever experienced this joy, you know how important spiritual blessings are—and how important it is for us to give the spiritual blessings priority when something happens to us that is not fair.

Future joy. Do you remember the first line in Donne's prayer?

> O eternal and most gracious God, you have reserved your perfect joy and perfect glory for the future.

We Christians are a people called to see not just time, but also eternity. The apostle Paul says in Romans 8:18, "I consider that our present sufferings are not worth comparing with the glory that will be revealed in us."

Paul's penetrating vision recognizes the transitory nature of this life. The frustrations we feel as we live in a universe in bondage to decay are only natural. The present universe is corrupt, and life here is bound to be unfair. But a day of liberation lies ahead. And when the day of liberation arrives, then "glory will be revealed in us."

Then, and then alone, will we know perfect joy. Then we will see clearly the beauty and the goodness of our God.

Until Then

Until then you and I, like all the rest of the human race, will simply have to deal with those things in life that are not fair. What, in addition to the practical suggestions I've included in each chapter, can we do to preserve our sense of the goodness of God even when life isn't fair?

(1) *We can recognize and welcome life's goats and chickens.* Most of the things we think of as not fair are really little things that will be with us only a little while.

It helps if we classify them as goats and chickens—annoyances rather than disasters. It helps, too, if, when they leave, we stop to appreciate how good life really is.

(2) *We can look for bright highlights even when days are dark.* It is so important to maintain perspective when something unfair happens to us. One way to do this is to look consciously for the good and, when we pray about our troubles, to thank God for our blessings. Cultivating gratitude not only honors the Lord but also makes difficulties more bearable.

Again, God doesn't expect us to give thanks *for* everything. But we are to give thanks *in* everything. The same Philippians passage goes on to add this important advice: "Finally, brothers, whatever is true, whatever is noble, whatever is right, whatever is pure, whatever is lovely, whatever is admirable—if anything is excellent or praiseworthy—think about such things" (Philippians 4:8).

(3) *Give priority to spiritual blessings.* You and I are vulnerable in this life. Sickness can strike any of us. Accidents can snatch our children from us. Others can defraud or cheat us. Life here truly is not fair.

But nothing that happens to us can threaten the spiritual blessings which we possess in Christ. Not trouble or hardship or persecution. Not famine or nakedness or danger or sword. Not death or life, not the present or the future. In Jesus Christ we have spiritual resources that no one can ever take from us. It is in these spiritual resources that we will find the strength to endure, and the grace to transcend the unfair, and even hidden springs of unexpected joy.

The apostle Peter puts it this way: "In [God's] great mercy he has given us new birth into a living hope through the resurrection of Jesus Christ from the dead, and into an inheritance that can never perish, spoil or fade—kept in heaven for you, who through faith are shielded by God's power until the coming of the salvation that is ready to be revealed in the last time. In this you greatly rejoice, though now for a little while you may have had to suffer in all kinds of trials. These have come so that your faith—of greater worth than gold, which perishes even though refined by fire—may be proved genuine and may result in praise, glory and honor when Jesus Christ is revealed. Though you have not seen him, you love him; and even though you do not see him now, you believe in him and are filled with an inexpressible and glorious joy, for you are receiving the goal of your faith, the salvation of your souls" (1 Peter 1:3–9).

(4) *Remain hopeful and expectant.* With the psalmist, most of us can be "confident of this: I will see the goodness of the Lord in the land of the living"(Psalm 27:13). Yet even when there is no prospect of relief, we Christians have an eternal hope. In Donne's words, God has "reserved your perfect joy and perfect glory for the future, when we will for the first time know you as we are known."

However unfair life may be to us now, the time is coming when we will fully appreciate the goodness of our God.

For Meditation and Discussion

1. Thinking back over the whole book, which of the chapters have been most relevant to your own experience?

2. In this final chapter the author makes several suggestions about putting the unfair in life in perspective. Which of the following seems most helpful to you?

   • The unfair should make us more appreciative of our normal blessings.

   • When life is unfair, it's important to be aware of highlights for which we can be thankful.

   • Nothing that happens to us can cause us to lose the spiritual blessings we have in Christ.

   • God has reserved complete joy for the future, when we know him as we are known and fully appreciate his goodness.